Strategic Management
Abridged Edition

Garth Saloner
Andrea Shepard
Joel Podolny

prepared for use in the
Graduate School of Business
University of Chicago

Copyright © 2001 by John Wiley & Sons, Inc.

All rights reserved.

Reproduction or translation of any part of this work beyond that permitted by Sections 107 and 108 of the 1976 United States Copyright Act without the permission of the copyright owner is unlawful. Requests for permission or further information should be addressed to the Permission Department, John Wiley & Sons.

Printed in the United States of America.

ISBN 0-471-43808-1

STRATEGIC MANAGEMENT

GARTH SALONER
Stanford University
Graduate School of Business

ANDREA SHEPARD
Stanford University
Graduate School of Business

JOEL PODOLNY
Stanford University
Graduate School of Business

JOHN WILEY & SONS, INC.
New York / Chichester / Weinheim / Brisbane / Singapore / Toronto

Executive Editor	Brent Gordon
Editor	Jeff Marshall
Developmental Editor	Johnna Barto
Marketing Manager	Jessica Garcia
Production Editor	Sandra Russell
Cover Illustrator	Mick Wiggins
Designer	Madelyn Lesure
Illustration Editor	Anna Melhorn
Production Management Services	Hermitage Publishing Services

This book was typeset in Janson by Hermitage Publishing Services and printed and bound by Courier Companies. The cover was printed by Lehigh Press, Inc.

The paper in this book was manufactured by a mill whose forest management programs include sustained yield harvesting of its timberlands. Sustained yield harvesting principles ensure that the number of trees cut each year does not exceed the amount of new growth.

This book is printed on acid-free paper. ∞

Copyright © 2001 by John Wiley & Sons, Inc. All rights reserved.

No part of this publication may be reproduced, stored in a retrieval system or transmitted in any form or by any means, electronic, mechanical, photocopying recording, scanning or otherwise, except as permitted under Sections 107 or 108 of the 1976 United States Copyright Act, without either the prior written permission of the Publisher or authorization through payment of the appropriate per-copy fee to the Copyright Clearance Center, 222 Rosewood Drive, Danvers, MA 01923, (508) 750-8400, fax (508) 750-4470. Requests to the Publisher for permission should be addressed to the Permissions Department, John Wiley & Sons, Inc. 605 Third Avenue, New York, NY 10158-0012, (212) 850-6008, E-mail: PERMREQ@WILEY.COM. To order books or for customer service call 1-800-CALL-WILEY (225-5945).

Library of Congress Cataloging in Publication Data

Saloner, Garth.
    Strategic management/Garth Saloner, Andrea Shepard, Joel Podolny.
        p. cm.
    Includes bibliographical references and index.
    ISBN 0-471-38071-7 (cloth: alk. paper)
    1. Strategic planning. I. Shepard, Andrea. II. Podolny, Joel M. (Joel Marc) III. Title.
HD30.28.S25 2001
658.4'021–dc21
                                                                                                                      00-043275

ISBN 0-471-38071-7

Printed in the United States of America.

10 9 8 7 6 5 4 3 2 1

CONTENTS

1 INTRODUCTION 1
  1.1 Strategic Management 1
  1.2 The Role of Business Strategy 2
    Examples: Dell Computer and Compaq Computer 4
    The Dynamics of Business Strategy 6
    Strategic Planning versus Strategic Thinking 8
  1.3 The Organization and Its Objectives 10
    Performance: Overarching Objectives 10
    Firms and Managers 12
  1.4 Perspectives on the Impact of the General Manager 14
  1.5 Organization of the Book 16

2 BUSINESS STRATEGY 19
  2.1 Introduction 19
  2.2 Describing Business Strategy 19
    Goals 20
    Scope 21
    Competitive Advantage 21
    Logic 22
  2.3 Relationship of Strategy to Mission, Purpose, Values, and Vision 24
    Mission, Purpose, and Values 24
    Vision 27
  2.4 The Strategy Statement 28
    Benefits of an Explicit Strategy Statement 29
    The Form and Use of the Strategy Statement 30
    An Example: Borders Books 31
  2.5 Developing Strategy: The Strategy Process 33
    Strategy Identification 34
    Strategy Evaluation: Testing the Logic 35
    Strategy Process and Strategic Change 36
  2.6 Summary 38

3 COMPETITIVE ADVANTAGE 39
  3.1 Introduction 39

- **3.2** Value and Competitive Advantage 39
- **3.3** Two Main Routes to Competitive Advantage 41
  - Position 43
  - Capabilities 46
- **3.4** Sustainable Competitive Advantage 48
  - Capability as Sustainable Competitive Advantage 49
  - Position as Sustainable Competitive Advantage 50
- **3.5** The Relationship of Position to Capabilities 51
- **3.6** Position, Capabilities, and "The Resource-Based View of the Firm" 53
- **3.7** The Cost-Quality Frontier and Competitive Advantage 55
  - Product Quality and Cost 56
  - A Cost-Quality Framework 58
  - Using the Cost-Quality Frontier to Illustrate Competitive Advantage: An Example 59
- **3.8** Summary 63

4 INTERNAL CONTEXT: ORGANIZATION DESIGN 65
- **4.1** Introduction 65
- **4.2** Organization Design and Competitive Advantage 65
- **4.3** Strategy and Organization at Southwest Airlines 67
  - Southwest's Strategy and Performance 67
  - Southwest's Organization 68
  - Comparisons to Other Airlines 70
  - Summary: Consistency and Alignment 71
- **4.4** The Challenge of Organization Design 71
  - The Coordination Problem 72
  - The Incentive Problem 73
- **4.5** Meeting the Challenge 75
  - Architecture: Structure 76
  - Architecture: Compensation and Rewards 82
  - Routines 86
  - Culture 88
- **4.6** ARC Analysis 89
- **4.7** Summary 90

5 ORGANIZATION AND COMPETITIVE ADVANTAGE 93
- **5.1** Introduction 93
- **5.2** Aligning Strategy and Organization 95
  - Applying ARC Analysis to Assess Strategic Alignment: Southwest Airlines Revisited 97
  - Other Examples: Sony, Apple Computer, and Silicon Graphics 101
- **5.3** **Building and Creating Competitive Advantage** 102

    Explorers and Exploiters **103**
    Interdependence and Tight-Coupling **106**
    Organizational Slack **109**
    Central Direction **110**
    The ARC of Explorers and Exploiters **111**
5.4 Combining Exploration and Exploitation **114**
5.5 Costs of Organizational Change **117**
5.6 Summary **117**

INDEX **429**

CHAPTER 1

INTRODUCTION

1.1 STRATEGIC MANAGEMENT

Some firms experience meteoric growth, achieving industry leadership, while others falter, stagnate, or fail. Some firms seem to seize every opportunity, while others seem always to move too late or not at all. Consider, for example, the performance of Coca-Cola relative to its contemporaries. One dollar invested in the Coca-Cola Company at its initial public offering in 1919 would have been worth over $200,000 in 2000, while a dollar invested in a portfolio of representative large U.S. stocks over the same period would have been worth less than $4200![1] Moreover, for every successful company started when Coca-Cola was founded, many more have long gone out of business.

A manager who is keenly aware of this tremendous range of firm performance naturally looks for some pattern that distinguishes success from failure. However, a review of the history of successful firms suggests a broad range of ways to achieve superior performance. Some firms have succeeded by innovating, and others by eschewing innovation in favor of operational efficiency. Some successful firms have sought to grow as quickly as possible, while others have pursued modest growth. Some dominate their market, while others prosper by concentrating on a small market segment.

Variation in firm performance and in the strategies successful firms pursue is not surprising given the vast differences in the industries in which firm participate, the regulatory environments they face, and the human, financial, and physical assets they can bring to bear. But the variation is perplexing for a manager who must navigate the firm's external environment in a way that makes the most of the firm's assets. Strategic management is fundamentally about helping the manager in that quest. It is about developing a set of tools and conceptual maps for uncovering the systematic relationships between the choices the manager makes and the performance the firm realizes.

---

[1] *Source: Stocks, Bonds, Bills, and Inflation: 1997 Yearbook* (Chicago: Ibbotson Associates, 1997) and authors' calculations.

Having a set of tools and frameworks is essential because a manager faces a bewildering array of choices every day. This array includes deciding which products or services to pursue, which investments to make, which human resource management policies to implement, and which organizational structures to adopt. Furthermore, in an organization of even modest size, strategic choices are made by multiple decision makers and implemented by many employees in different functional areas and geographies.

There is the danger, then, that the course the firm takes will be determined by the buffeting it receives from its competitive environment and by the aggregation of uncoordinated decisions made by independent actors within the firm. Its performance will be haphazard, opportunities will be lost, and threats will loom uncountered. The alternative is for the firm's managers to develop a common, overall sense of what they want the business to achieve and to formulate a strategy that they believe will enable it to achieve those goals. Developing and implementing a strategy that allows managers to exercise more control over the firm's direction and to chart a course that enhances the firm's performance are the objectives of strategic management.

1.2 THE ROLE OF BUSINESS STRATEGY

Firm performance depends both on the actions the firm takes and on the context in which those actions are taken. By "action" we mean the acquisition and deployment of the firm's assets. Each firm has some existing set of assets including know-how, business processes, plant and equipment, brand equity, formal and informal organizational structure, financial resources, and so forth. Action consists of deploying existing assets and acquiring new ones. Although many of these decisions are routine and incremental, some asset acquisition and deployment decisions can profoundly affect the firm.[2] For example, in an attempt to improve its performance in the small car segment of the automobile industry, General Motors (GM) decided in the early 1980s to invest more than a *billion* dollars in a new, small car division it named "Saturn." Saturn represented a sharp break with the product development, manufacturing, distribution, and human resources management processes common to GM's other divisions. The shift represented by Saturn was embodied in significant redeployment of GM's human resources, a change in its fundamental business practices, and a major investment of its financial assets in a new plant.

Although the firm chooses the actions it takes, factors that are immutable, at least in the short run, also affect its performance. These factors represent the "context" in which the firm acts. As our discussion of "action" suggests, some of these factors are internal. The firm's *internal context* consists of the assets it owns and the way it is organized.[3] Other factors are external to the firm. The firm's *external environment* includes

---

[2] This perspective is consistent with the focus of Pankaj Ghemawat who describes the firm's major resource *commitments* as its major strategic assets. (*Source:* Pankaj Ghemawat, *Commitment: The Dynamics of Strategy*, New York: Free Press, 1991.)

[3] It is tempting to include the way the firm is organized as an asset rather than as a separate feature of its internal context. Instead we choose to preserve organization as a separate category to highlight the complex and important role it plays in affecting firm performance. Because organization determines the way people interact, the activities they choose to pursue, and the policies and routines the firm employs to get things done, we believe that the organizational attributes of the firm deserve separate mention.

both industry characteristics—such as actual and potential competitors, buyers, and suppliers—as well as nonmarket factors, such as the regulatory, political, and social environment in which the firm operates.

The firm's actions and the context in which they are taken *together* determine performance as Figure 1-1 illustrates. Note that, instead of separate arrows from context and action to performance, the arrows in the figure merge to represent this codetermination of performance. Context and action can combine to determine performance in several ways. Typically, the actions that managers take are importantly conditioned by the context they face. For example, the stance that government regulators take toward mergers and acquisitions affects a firm's ability to change its scope. Or the product development behavior of rival firms might affect the performance of a firm that has decided to delay its new product line. Sometimes the actions the firm takes contribute to shaping its context, as when a firm completes an acquisition that alters its rivals' market behavior. In either case, the performance the firm achieves is a product of both its context and its action.

There is no simple prescription for action that will work in most situations because the relationship between action and context is complex. Actions that are stunningly effective in one context may fail abysmally in another. As a result, managers need to understand how context mediates the effect of action on performance. This understanding allows the manager to assess how a competitor's introduction of new products or repositioning of its existing product line will affect the firm's own competitive position, for example, or to determine what new capabilities the business needs to acquire to take advantage of new market opportunities, the kinds of financial returns the firm should expect from expanding capacity, or whether it is worth investing in that new technology the engineers have been recommending.

More generally, understanding these interactions enables general managers to assess whether the kinds of actions the firm has been taking, and currently contemplates taking, are likely to result in the performance management would like to achieve. One goal of strategic management is to provide the conceptual frameworks that will help a manager understand the key relationships among actions, context, and performance. These frameworks are designed to answer the question "What actions will be most likely to achieve the organization's goals given its internal and external context?"

Answering this question is essential to formulating a potentially successful strategy, but it is not enough. It is not enough for the manager to know what kinds of

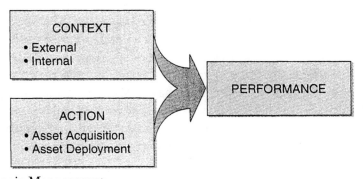

FIGURE 1-1 Strategic Management

actions are likely to lead to success. The general manager must also have some way to communicate that understanding to the rest of the organization. Because the general manager does not make the thousands of decisions that, in aggregate, determine the success or failure of the firm, he or she must articulate a framework, plan, or approach for the firm to guide the many specific decisions that must be made as the business goes forward. This is the role of strategy. A strategy reflects the manager's understanding of the key relationships among actions, context, and performance and is crafted to guide the firm's many decision makers to take actions that are consistent with that understanding. Helping managers formulate and implement such a strategy is central to strategic management as a normative field.

We want to stress that a strategy, as the term is used here, may not (in general, does not) specify any particular action. A strategy will not specify the tactics that should be used to implement it. A manager generally cannot describe all the possible contextual elements that the firm might encounter and all the relevant actions that it might consider taking. Even if this were feasible, a lengthy, detailed analysis would be difficult to communicate to all the relevant decision makers within the firm and not terribly useful for those who must implement a consistent plan of action.

Rather, the strategy defines a framework for guiding the choice of actions. It is a broad articulation of the kinds of products the organization will produce, the basis on which its products will compete with those of its competitors, and the types of resources and capabilities the firm must have or develop to implement the strategy successfully. A strategy in this sense is the starting point for developing a detailed action plan, but it transcends the specifics of any particular plan.

We stress this particular interpretation of strategy to distinguish it from the many different ways the word "strategy" frequently is used in business settings. For example, it is common usage to pose questions such as "What was Jim's strategy in negotiating the new contract with his client?" or "What was Kodak's strategy in addressing the threat from Fuji?" Although these are legitimate uses of the word "strategy" (and indeed, we will sometimes slip into this usage in later chapters), they do not correspond to the way we are using the term here. These uses refer to the means for achieving a limited objective. We are using the term to encompass an overall approach to a business.

Examples: Dell Computer and Compaq Computer

To illustrate how strategy can frame a firm's actions, compare the strategies of Dell and Compaq at the turn of the century. Both firms are leading manufacturers of personal computers, but they have very different strategies. Dell focuses primarily on direct sales of customized, personal computers to end-users. By selling directly to the end-user, Dell can have very low distribution costs. It can customize computers at low cost because it produces to order, avoiding a large inventory of finished goods. As a complement to production-to-order, Dell has established a supply chain management system that enables it to order components shortly before they are actually needed rather than carrying them in inventory. Because the cost of computer components often declines with time, just-in-time component acquisition enables Dell to keep its manufacturing costs low.

Because Dell can keep its manufacturing and distribution costs low while rapidly producing customized computers, it can offer customers an attractive product and service at very competitive prices. The high demand that this creates enables Dell to reap manufacturing and distribution scale efficiencies, driving unit costs lower still. To summarize, the essence of Dell's strategy has been selling customized computers directly to end-users, minimizing the time from placement of customer order to ultimate fulfillment, while offering attractive prices supported by low manufacturing and distribution costs. This strategy is reflected in Dell's advertising message: "At Dell, we believe nothing should stand between you and us. Want a clear path to success?"[4]

Another leading personal computer manufacturer, Compaq Computer, has adopted a quite different strategy. Two of Compaq's acquisitions exemplify the difference between Compaq and Dell. The first was Compaq's purchase of Tandem Computer, a manufacturer of "fault-tolerant" computers for firms, such as financial institutions and insurance companies, for whom business interruptions caused by the computer "going down" are particularly costly. The other was Compaq's acquisition of Digital Equipment Corporation (DEC), one of the most significant producers of midrange computers in the pre-PC era. One of the key assets that DEC brought to Compaq was its services and support organization. Through its history of selling to large corporate customers, DEC has developed significant know-how in helping its customers use information technology to solve their business problems. With these acquisitions, Compaq has positioned itself as a computer company with a broad range of computer products and the know-how to help its business customers deploy those products to meet their business needs. Consistent with this strategy, Compaq's advertising sends a different message from Dell's, rhetorically posing the question: "Who's at the hub of today's most important strategic IT partnerships?"[5]

Each of these quite different strategies provides the management of Dell and Compaq with a *framework* to guide their future choice of actions. In Dell's case, for example, one expects to see actions directed toward cost-cutting and ensuring that end-users' points of contact with the company, such as its Web site, are robust, user-friendly, and efficient. In Compaq's case, one expects to see efforts aimed at producing robust technologies that interact in networks suitable for deployment by large corporate customers. Although it would be virtually impossible for the firms' managers to describe fully the actions these firms should take as a function of all the contextual elements they might face, their strategies outline an overall approach to the personal computer business that is a valuable guide to decision making.

These two companies are pursuing different strategies, even though they face many common contextual factors. Because both manufacture computers, both are susceptible to trends in demand for computing as well as to changes in computer technology. They also face many of the same competitors and potential competitors. Both are affected by a common nonmarket environment.

Despite these similarities, there are also differences in their contexts that provide some hints as to why they might be pursuing different strategies. For one, each faces

---

[4] *Time*, July 6, 1998, p. 57.
[5] *Fortune*, July 20, 1998, p. 13.

the other as a competitor, so their competitive environments differ! As we will emphasize later, firms can sometimes enhance performance by differentiating their products and services from those of their major competitors. More importantly perhaps, through their years in business, Dell and Compaq have developed different internal contexts: different workforces, areas of technical expertise, corporate cultures, brand awareness, abilities to adapt to changing market and technological conditions, financial positions, and so on. Their different internal contexts suggest that they might successfully pursue different strategies.

Although it is not possible to assess the likelihood that these strategies will be successful without more analysis, some features of their contexts can be identified that may be key determinants of success or failure. Compaq, for example, is responding to a void created by the failure of many of the large vertically integrated computer companies of the mainframe era, which had previously helped large companies solve their information technology problems. Its success will depend on the demand for these services and the extent to which it can meet that demand. Compaq is also betting that it has the organizational ability to integrate its merger partners successfully. For its part, Dell is relying both on having a first-mover advantage with this strategy, so that it faces no immediate serious competition from rivals pursuing similar strategies, and on its ability to stay ahead of emerging competitors as they learn from Dell's success.

Although we have only scratched the surface of these companies' strategies, these examples give a glimpse of what fuller descriptions might entail and what the utility of a comprehensive strategy would be. A strategy describes a framework for charting a course of action. It explicates an approach for the company that builds on its strengths and is a good fit with the firm's external environment. Because the strategy is succinct, it is easy to communicate within and outside the firm and is a good guide for the managers who have to implement it. Moreover, by explaining how the firm intends to succeed given the context it faces, the strategy alerts management to the assumptions about the firm's context that are essential for the strategy's success. This information enables them to interpret contextual changes, anticipating how these changes might affect the firm's performance.

The Dynamics of Business Strategy

Because the firm's internal and environmental context changes over time, so too does the efficacy of a given strategy. Consequently, the idea that strategy is dynamic is inherent in our conception of strategic management. Indeed, the impetus for a change in the firm's deployment and acquisition of its assets is frequently a change in the context in which it operates. In a stable environment, strategic analysis tends to take a back seat to efficient, effective implementation. When simply "doing more of the same" is clearly insufficient, however, strategy and strategic change quickly become a focus of managerial attention.

The GM example introduced earlier illustrates this idea. The development of the Saturn division was motivated in part by a growing view inside GM that its current methods of designing, producing, and selling cars were causing it to lose ground against other, primarily Japanese, auto manufacturers. Organizational structures in which design, manufacturing, and marketing were largely separate and independent processes led to very long cycle times (the time from conception of a vehicle to the production of the first car) and final products that were unresponsive to customer preferences. Adversarial relations between management and the United Auto Workers union resulted in high labor costs and inflexible manufacturing processes. The organization and incentive structure of the dealer network led to adversarial customer–dealer relations. The company's top management viewed the resulting loss of competitive advantage as a major strategic issue. They recognized that the set of actions appropriate in the old context was no longer effective.

Many forces for change act on the firm's external environment. Some of these are fairly predictable, such as the changes that typically occur as an industry goes through a life cycle from inception through growth, maturity, and decline. Other changes are less predictable and result from underlying changes in the demand and supply conditions facing the industry. For example, globalization may change the nature of competition in a previously domestic industry as foreign firms enter the market. The entry of Asian and European automobile manufacturers into the United States dramatically affected GM's competitive position. Or the industry may consolidate as rival companies merge, thereby changing the nature of competition. The current wave of mergers in telecommunications, for example, is restructuring competition in the global telecom market. Technological change may affect the firm's strategic situation as when the Internet makes it possible for individuals to trade stocks and book airline tickets at low cost from home, thereby threatening the cherished relationships between brokers and customers and travel agents and clients. Changes in the nonmarket environment, such as deregulation of financial institutions in the United States, alter the strategic context of existing industry participants as well as potential entrants. As Figure 1-2 illustrates, all such changes affect the efficacy of the firm's strategy. To be able to react in a timely manner, firms have to understand the potential impact of these changes.

The firm's strategic and environmental context can also change as a result of its own actions. Figure 1-2 shows change initiated by the company as the arrow from action to context. Sometimes a firm *deliberately* acts to change its context. A company, for example, may decide to acquire new resources to address a new business objective, thereby changing the firm's strategic assets. Compaq's acquisition of Tandem Computer is a good example of this. Similarly, a firm can take actions to change its external environment. Kodak, for example, has invested heavily in seeking the intervention of U.S. trade policy to enhance its competitive position in camera film in Japan. Around 1900, huge corporations like Standard Oil and U.S. Steel were formed by managers intent on concentrating control of whole industries under a single management. Software firms engage in alliances intended to influence the emergence of industry standards and, therefore, their stature as standard bearers.

Sometimes, however, the changes created by the firms are *unanticipated*. Companies may find an opportunity to exploit new technologies produced as unintended byproducts of their R&D programs. Or strategic alliances may open new, unexpected opportunities for the firm to pursue new markets. Some firms are adept at exploiting these opportunities as they arise, while others allow them to slip away. 3-M, for example, is renowned for its ability to move effectively to develop a wide range of innova-

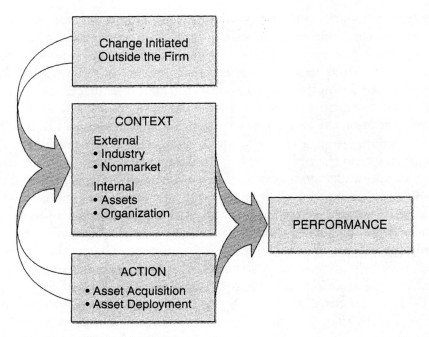

FIGURE 1-2 Dynamics of Business Strategy

tions. In contrast, IBM and Xerox suffer from a legacy of failing to capture value from the ancillary innovations created in their research labs. In some particularly dramatic cases, the changes wrought by incumbent firms have unexpectedly swept the incumbents aside. The Swiss watch industry, for example, developed quartz technology only to discover that the industry as it was organized—with many specialist producers of individual components—was ill-suited to commercializing the technology. As a result, Swiss leadership of the industry was (temporarily) ceded to Japanese firms. Intentionally or not, firms can be agents of change.

Strategic Planning versus Strategic Thinking

As already asserted, formulating and implementing strategy require that a general manager have a cognitive map of the relationships among actions, context, and performance. The manager must understand current sources of performance, the threats and opportunities presented by changes inside and outside the firm, and how to change course in response to them. How the firm obtains the necessary information to develop and maintain that map, formulate and change strategy, and communicate the strategy within the organization is termed *strategy process*.

Most mature companies have a systematic, formal *strategic planning* routine as their strategy process. Although there is substantial variation in who is involved in such a process and how it is carried out, we can describe the general features of a typical formal strategic planning process. Strategic planning is discussed in more detail later in the book, but it is useful to provide a rough sketch here to distinguish between strategic *planning* and the kind of strategic *thinking* that is the focus of this book.

A strategic planning process in a mature company is typically conducted on an annual cycle and often involves the development of an annual and, perhaps, multiyear business plan. In firms with multiple business units, each unit is asked to develop a plan for itself, and those plans get reviewed, revised, and aggregated by more senior managers as the plan "moves up" the organization. The content of a strategic plan is typically some combination of the strategic analysis described here and an operating plan and budget. For example, a strategic plan for a business unit at General Electric (GE), a company renowned for its strategic planning processes, was described as having the following elements in the early 1980s:

- Identification and formulation of environmental assumptions of strategic importance,
- Identification and in-depth analysis of competitors, including assumptions about their probable strategies,
- Analysis of the [unit's] own resources,
- Development and evaluation of strategy alternatives,
- Preparation of the [unit's] strategic plan, including estimates of capital spending for the next five years,
- Preparation of the [unit's] operating plan, which detailed the next year of the [unit's] strategic plan.[6]

This list sensibly covers many issues that should be thought about in formulating business unit strategy. But the strategic planning process in many companies also has several characteristics that make it an ineffective tool for strategic thinking. First, there is often a mismatch between the timing of the planning process and the dynamics of strategic change. In many cases, the firm's strategy is more durable than any specific business or strategic plan. Although the strategy may be "tweaked" now and then in response to critical changes in the elements of Figure 1-2, it is not uncommon for its essential characteristics to survive many planning periods and, hence, many annual plans. In other cases, environmental change is so rapid that the formulation of static annual plans to which managers must adhere impedes the firm's ability to respond in time.

A second type of problem firms encounter is the nature of the review process. We will have much more to say about this later, but participants in these processes typically report that the review process is cumbersome and replete with incentives for playing company politics. The timing and review problems together have prompted many companies, particularly new, high-technology firms, to eschew formal strategic planning processes in favor of a more fluid and dynamic approach to strategy formulation.

A final, and critical, problem that many companies have encountered in implementing a formal planning process is that most of the emphasis tends to be placed on

---

[6] Francis J. Aguilar and Richard Hamermesh, "General Electric: Strategic Position—1981," Harvard Business School Case, 381–174.

the budget and operating plans. In GE's process, for example, the budget and operating plan are only two of the six basic elements. In practice, however, GE and other companies have found that these elements, particularly the capital budget, consume the bulk of managerial attention. The other elements are at the heart of strategic thinking but get short shrift. The reason for this is that the strategic plan is as much a part of the political process of resource allocation within the firm as it is an attempt to think creatively about business unit strategy. Indeed, GE later amended its strategic planning process to provide much more emphasis on coherent explication of strategy and less on preparing detailed plans and budgets.

In this book we are more concerned with discussing tools and ideas for rigorously formulating strategy than with the planning process *per se*. We are concerned with general managers' ability to develop and maintain a conceptual map of their businesses that ties together the elements of Figure 1-2, to conceptualize a strategy, and then to think through, "on their feet," the impact of changes in their internal and external environment. We call this *strategic thinking* rather than strategic planning, and it is our main focus.

One reason for our focus on strategic thinking is that many general managers do not have the luxury of spending long periods of time in reflective, detailed, strategic planning. A more compelling reason, however, is that we believe strategic thinking is critical to achieving the firm's objectives and that embedding it in a formal planning process too often obscures rather than enhances strategic thought. We also believe that boards of directors and senior management are increasingly demanding that their general managers think strategically. They want their managers to have a mental model of the business they run that consists of a comprehensive understanding of the forces at work in Figure 1-2 as well as a strategy that provides a framework for translating that understanding into action. Most of the book is therefore devoted to providing such a manager with the tools and frameworks necessary for building a mental model and developing a strategy. We do, however, return to the subject of strategic planning in Chapter 15, where we discuss integrating strategic thinking with a strategic planning process.

1.3 THE ORGANIZATION AND ITS OBJECTIVES

So far, we have talked about "firms," "performance," and "managers" as if these concepts were clearly defined. Before proceeding, however, we need to clarify what we mean by performance, the kinds of organizations to which strategic management can be applied, and the managers who might most benefit from understanding strategic management.

Performance: Overarching Objectives

Figures 1-1 and 1-2 describe the outcome of the firm's action plan as "performance." There are many possible measures of firm performance, including market share, reputation, innovation, brand image, profitability, employee satisfaction, and so on. In striving to formulate strategy to improve firm performance, managers need to be clear about which of these performance dimensions they hope to affect. Often a firm's strategy is couched in terms of excelling on a particular dimension. For example, the firm may have a stated objective of achieving a dominant position in the market in which it competes or of being the highest quality producer, or the most innovative firm in the industry. Under the leadership of Jack Welch, for example, one of GE's stated goals was to be "number one or two" in every market in which it competed.

Yet a goal like being "number one or number two" or the most innovative is typically not the ultimate goal of the firm. The ultimate goal is profitability. The directors of for-profit firms have a fiduciary responsibility to the firm's shareholders, and these investors are interested primarily in receiving as high a return as possible. Dominating the industry or producing the highest quality product can be a useful description of how the firm's managers hope to maximize the firm's profit, but it should not be confused with the firm's ultimate goal. Apple Computer, for example, discovered that producing the highest quality computer hardware possible was not the way for it to maximize profit. The firm's managers were slow to come to this conclusion because they confused the strategic goal—great hardware products—with the firm's overarching objective: maximize profit. When the strategic goal no longer enhances profits, it should be changed. In what follows, therefore, we assume that profit-maximization is the firm's overarching objective.

We take this to be a reasonable description of reality in many, but certainly not all, for-profit organizations. In practice there are two main sets of reasons why behavior may deviate from the pursuit of this goal. The first is that even a for-profit firm may have been established with a social goal as an explicit objective. Shareholders may have invested (and continue to invest) knowing that they are sacrificing some monetary gain in exchange for progress on the social objective. Patagonia, for example, is a California-based company devoted to producing outdoor hiking, climbing, and camping equipment that is environmentally friendly. The company's devotion to the environment may well make it a less profitable enterprise, since it devotes resources to activities that other companies without those concerns might not.

The second reason the firm might not pursue wealth-maximization is that the goals of managers at for-profit organizations are not necessarily the same as those of the owners. Self-interested managers may pursue activities that are in their own, but not necessarily the shareholders', best interests. For example, a manager may be inclined to take actions that boost short-run at the expense of long run profitability if that could lead to a promotion. Or managers may pursue personal power and influence at the expense of organizational performance. For a variety of reasons explored later in this book, shareholders have problems preventing this kind of self-serving behavior.

To the extent that organizations can and do define their overarching goals differently from profit-maximization, they must recognize those differences in formulating and implementing strategy. To the extent that firms define their overarching goal in terms of profit-maximization but deviate from that pursuit because of the personal agendas of the actors within the firm, strategy formulation and implementation must be sensitive to issues of politics, influence, and incentives inside the firm. For example, managers who want to direct the firm's resources toward a new product position may encounter resistance from engineers whose compensation depends on patent output and the rate of new product development. Redirection may be good for the firm but bad for the productivity of key engineers. We will return to the issue of designing the organization to account for incentive problems and internal conflict in Chapter 4.

The view that profit-maximization is the appropriate overall objective is clearly inappropriate for private nonprofit and public organizations. For these organizations, strategic thinking often involves defining their overall objective. Private nonprofit and public organizations are "owned" by their customers and/or the larger community, and the organizations' objectives must reflect those interests. Once ownership is established and the interests of the owners are defined, however, the role of management—as in the for-profit environment—is to promote those objectives as effectively as possible. For this endeavor, the same principles that guide strategy formulation in the for-profit world are also appropriate for these organizations.

Firms and Managers

We have been speaking about devising a strategy that could enhance the performance of the "firm." In doing so, we have glossed over the tremendous variation in the scope and complexity of businesses. Some firms operate (almost exclusively) in a single business: Genentech is a pharmaceutical firm, Dell is a computer firm, Coca-Cola was, for much of its history, a purveyor of Coke. For these companies, there is a good match between what we have been calling a firm and a business. For these firms it makes sense to talk about an external context, internal assets, and the interaction that leads to performance. But many companies consist of a number of disparate lines of business, each of which has a distinct external context and set of strategic assets. How can one strategy be appropriate for this entire set of businesses? How can one talk about a mental map of the relationship among external context, internal context, and performance for a firm like ABB whose products range from financial services to railroad rolling stock to large power generators? Or a Hewlett-Packard that makes Unix servers, laser printers, and ink jet printers?

The answer, of course, is that one cannot. Strategic thinking requires you to describe the industry and the internal assets to which the strategy applies. For example, Hewlett-Packard has a Unix server business, an ink jet printer business, a laser printer business, and so on. Each of those businesses includes a number of products in a product line that is logically grouped together and constitutes a business unit. One can think about formulating a strategy for Hewlett-Packard's ink jet printer business or its Unix server business. But no single strategy will apply to both of these business units. Each unit has distinct assets that it brings to its business, and each has a distinct market environment in which it competes. If we were to detail the characteristics of the internal and external environments for each unit, we would describe two different "firms" that are part of a single company. For this reason, the strategy literature traditionally distinguishes between "business unit strategy" and "corporate strategy." This distinction is not important for the many small firms who operate in a single line of business, but it is important for companies competing in more than one industry. We will turn to the topic of corporate strategy in Chapter 14, but most of this book will be about business unit strategy.

Because we are focusing on business unit strategy, the "manager" we have in mind as our strategic thinker is the individual (or team) with responsibility for setting the direction for the business unit as a whole. This general manager sets the strategic direction and goals of the business, typically with input from subordinates, and integrates and coordinates the functional areas within it to achieve those goals. To do this effectively, the general manager needs to understand the functional areas for the business he or she manages. However, the general manager's role is not simply to oversee those functional areas but rather to set the strategic direction and goals for the business that serve as a guide for functional area policies.

Most companies have many general managers. Among the most senior management of the firm's business units are those who have ultimate responsibility for their overall strategic direction and who therefore, by definition, are general managers. However, it is incorrect to equate "senior" and "general." There are many senior managers (e.g., the chief financial officer) whose responsibilities do not include strategic responsibility for a business unit. On the other hand, managers much lower in the hierarchy often do have general management responsibilities. The principles of strategic management examined in this book are relevant to all general managers, regardless of their position in the firm.

This view of the strategic responsibility of general managers does not imply that strategic thinking consumes their day-to-day lives. Nor does it imply that strategic thinking is the activity on which general managers spend the most time. Indeed, it is not. As documented convincingly by Mintzberg,[7] the general manager fulfills a variety of roles, including performing ceremonial duties, acting as a company spokesperson, allocating resources, and dealing with day-to-day crises. However, even if one would not describe general managers primarily as strategic thinkers from observing their day-to-day activities, their decision making can drive the strategy of their organizations. A firm's strategy is in fact determined, consciously or unconsciously, by the decisions made by its general managers.

Implicit in this general management perspective is the idea that general managers can make a difference in firm performance. Indeed, the underlying premise of this book is that the deliberate coordination of the organization's acquisition and deployment activities can have a significant, positive effect on the probability that the organization will achieve its objectives. This may seem like a logical position for a strategic management text, and, ultimately, we believe that it is. But it is not uncontroversial, and some elements of the controversy suggest important limitations of this underlying premise. We will take these limitations seriously in later chapters and so briefly describe the source of them here.

---

[7] Henry Mintzberg, "The Manager's Job: Folklore and Fact," *Harvard Business Review* (July–August 1975), 49–61.

1.4 PERSPECTIVES ON THE IMPACT OF THE GENERAL MANAGER

The view of general manager as strategist evokes the image of the "captain of the ship" selecting the business unit's destination, setting its course, guiding it through unexpected storms, and shouting commands to the crew. Several criticisms of this view have been proposed, and, indeed, this view of management seems much too simplistic. Here, we review some of the primary perspectives on how managers affect performance and then summarize the perspective we adopt.

One clear problem with the "captain of the ship" view of strategy is that there is tremendous variety in who is involved in the strategy process. Small firms and those in rapidly changing high-technology markets often have quite centralized strategic decision making. Many other organizations have more participatory strategy-setting processes in which several layers of management are involved in gathering, analyzing, and drawing strategic conclusions from relevant data. This process helps build a common knowledge base and goals among the many managers in a complex organization. However, even though the process resembles the "captain of the ship" imagery much less in these organizations than it does in a small organization because the process is more participatory, ultimate responsibility for strategy typically rests with the senior general management of the business unit.

A more radical criticism is that the "captain of the ship" view ascribes far too large a role for managers in the fortunes of the organizations they lead and presents too rational and organized a view of how strategic change occurs. In this view, even a manager with a clear idea about where the firm should go has only limited ability to determine the firm's direction. The limitation arises through some combination of inertia and limited rationality. Inertia implies that the firm's internal context is difficult to change. Limited rationality means that it is hard for managers to have a clear, precise view of the path the firm should follow.

The strongest form of this criticism is associated with evolutionary economics and organizational ecology, where, it is argued, firms engage in behavior that is largely routine rather than purposive or strategic.[8] In a stable environment, an industry is populated by firms with routines that are well adapted to the environment. The surviving firms are all well adapted because firms that were not have failed. If the environment changes, the performance of the existing firms will be determined by how well their routines fit with the new environment. Existing organizations that happen to have routines that are also well adapted to the new environment do well. Others suffer and fail because their existing routines are not effective in the new environment, and they are unable to adapt. In this view, adaptation means mimicking the routines of the (accidentally) well-adapted firms, a process that is extremely risky and impeded by the existence of well-entrenched, tacit routines. As older, less-well adapted firms fail, new, better-adapted firms, born without the baggage of the old routines, replace them. In the most extreme interpretation of this evolutionary view, general managers deserve little of the credit for

---

[8] See, for example, Michael Hannan and John Freeman, *Organizational Ecology* (Cambridge, MA: Harvard University Press, 1989).

success or failure. Success is determined not by the firm purposively developing a strategy that fits its internal and external context but by the incidental fit of fairly inert firms to their environments.

Some scholars have argued for an intermediate approach. For example, Brian Quinn[9] argues that "the processes used to arrive at the total strategy are typically fragmented, evolutionary, and largely intuitive." He argues that strategy processes are best described by "logical incrementalism" in which relatively minor changes in strategy are made in response to changes in external conditions in an evolutionary and adaptive manner. Thus his view accommodates both an evolutionary view of strategic change and a role for senior management in incremental change. Similarly, Nelson and Winter[10] have argued that firms can be seen as a collection of routines that are largely tacit knowledge. When a routine fails, the firm searches for a modification or a substitute, but this search will not, in general, lead to an optimal change and may fail completely.

Robert Burgelman propounds another intermediate view.[11] Like Quinn, he emphasizes evolutionary change. However, he ascribes a more activist, explicit, and effective role for senior managers in setting the strategic direction of the firm. He argues that reasonably complex organizations (a category that includes most firms) are subject to both evolutionary and planned processes. In his view, at any point in time, senior management is responsible for articulating a strategy that is consistent with the strategic context the firm faces. Over time, however, other managers in the organization take actions that change the internal strategic context. For example, they may discover new product opportunities, improve manufacturing processes, or invent new technologies. If the internal changes are profound, the actual strategy the firm is implementing may be changed. The responsibility of senior managers is to recognize that the change has affected or might affect the firm's strategy, determine whether the change should be encouraged or resisted, and, if embraced, alter the firm's official strategy to accommodate the change.

These different views suggest quite different roles for general managers in the formulation of strategy and for strategy itself. We lean more towards a view of the world in which general managers and the strategies they formulate can and do make a difference. This book reflects that bias. At the same time, we see merit in the criticisms posed by these other perspectives and attempt to incorporate relevant insights from those views in our approach. We recognize, for example, that there are limits to how much management can control the fate of the firm. Environmental change cannot be fully foreseen and, even when recognized, cannot be fully offset by the actions/decisions of management. In short, luck matters. The best strategy cannot *guarantee* good performance.

---

[9] James Brian Quinn, "Strategic Change: 'Logical Incrementalism,'" *Sloan Management Review* 20 (Fall 1978), 7–21.

[10] R R. Nelson and S. Winter, *An Evolutionary Theory of Economic Change* (Cambridge, MA: Harvard University Press, 1982).

[11] Robert A. Burgelman, "A Model of the Interaction of Strategic Behavior, Corporate Context, and the Concept of Strategy," *Academy of Management Review* 8 (1983), 61–70.

Moreover, we recognize that being well adapted frequently carries a cost: Adaptation is a two-edged sword. In a stable environment, a firm takes actions over time that make it well adapted to its current environment but limit its ability to change should the need arise. Consequently, a firm that is the best at some narrowly defined task may find itself suddenly at a competitive disadvantage when the environment no longer rewards excellence in that task. Sometimes this creeps up on firms as they incrementally adapt to their environment; sometimes it is part of a conscious tradeoff between being efficient at what the firm is currently doing and being organized to foresee and manage change well.

Fundamental change is difficult. One reason for this is that firms develop routines that are spread throughout the organization and are difficult to change. In addition to the inertia from routines, change is difficult because there are always constituencies within the firm for whom the change is not beneficial and who will resist it. As a result, top management's declaration that the firm will change does not make change happen. To return to our captain of the ship metaphor, shouting orders has little effect if the crew is not listening.

Not only does the "top" of the organization often find it difficult to mandate change, but the unauthorized and unanticipated actions of lower management and/or operational personnel may profoundly affect the performance of the firm. As a consequence, strategy process is complex. An approach to strategic management that envisions strategy as simply a decision problem undertaken by a few analysts neglects the complex processes through which strategy is formulated, evaluated, and modified in organizations.

In short, it is a mistake to assume that strategy is a simple process in which a decision maker analyzes the situation, chooses the best course of action, and implements it. Although dispassionate analysis is crucial, so too is understanding the organizational context within which, and the process by which, strategy evolves. In this book we attempt to balance an analytical "top-down" approach to strategy with one that recognizes the complexities of the strategy process in practice. Strategic thinkers must appreciate that they cannot control fully the future of the organization. However, management does get to place bets in the deployment and acquisition of its assets. Understanding the strategic determinants of performance will help management place better bets but will not eliminate all the uncertainties the organization faces. Moreover, since the locus of strategy is often dispersed through the organization, the strategic thinker must understand the constraints on strategic change that the organization of the firm imposes. To maximize the likelihood of success as the firm's strategy evolves, managers must also understand how to alter the way the firm is organized and behaves. The alternative is to relegate strategic thinking to crisis management. Discovering in the middle of a typhoon that the crew has redesigned the navigation systems is not conducive to setting and following an optimal course.

1.5 ORGANIZATION OF THE BOOK

The first five chapters of this book are about strategy and the internal context of the firm. In Chapter 2 we define what we mean by "strategy" and describe the essential elements a strategy should have. We also discuss some related concepts, such as mission, vision, purpose, values, and so on. In Chapter 3, we turn to the issue of creating competitive advantage by leveraging the firm's capabilities or achieving an advantageous position. We also discuss the problem of sustaining competitive advantage in the face of competition and imitation by rivals.

With this basic understanding of strategy and competitive advantage established, we turn to the organization of the firm. Competitive advantage is achieved when a firm has a strategy that draws on the strengths of the firm's internal context. Although many views of strategy depict this context primarily as the firm's assets (its human and physical capital), we believe that the way these assets are organized is at least as important. In Chapters 4 and 5, therefore, we focus on the role of organization in firm performance and the relationship of organization design to strategy and strategic change. We begin by defining the fundamental problems of coordination and incentives that the organization design must resolve and how the solution achieved by the firm must align with its strategy. We then turn to a more dynamic view of organization design, exploring the tension between organization design that is well suited to taking advantage of the firm's current environment and a design that is appropriate for responding to and creating change in the firm's environment.

In Chapters 6–9, we examine the "environmental context" part of Figure 1-2. In particular, we examine the impact that the characteristics of the firm's industry have on its performance. Chapter 6 introduces our framework for analyzing the characteristics of a firm's external context that affect its ability to create and capture value. Chapter 7 provides an overview of the effects of competition on performance and explores the opportunities for mitigating competition through product differentiation. Chapter 8 examines competition in markets where the nature of competition is determined by the behavior of the major players in the industry and provides a framework for thinking about competitive interaction. Since the number and size distribution of firms are critical factors in determining the strength of competition, Chapter 9 discusses entry and barriers to entry.

Chapter 10 discusses the firm's position within its value chain, exploring how the structure of the value chain affects its relationships with buyers and suppliers and how it can create and capture value. Chapter 10 also provides a bridge to Chapters 11–13 where we move to an examination of the "change arrows" in Figure 1-2. In particular, in Chapter 11 we look at issues that arise as industries evolve and firms undertake strategic actions to alter their external context. In Chapter 12 we apply these ideas to industries like electronic commerce, telecommunications, and others that are characterized by network effects or demand-side increasing returns. We then discuss globalization. Increasingly, the fact that they compete in a global economy is a crucial aspect of many firms' strategic context. In Chapter 13, we examine the challenges and opportunities of developing and implementing strategy in a global context.

In Chapter 14 we turn our attention to strategy in large multibusiness firms, the subject known as corporate strategy. This chapter discusses how the corporate office might add value to the firm's constituent businesses. We discuss the difference between corporate and business strategy and the avenues available for enhancing business unit performance.

Finally, in Chapter 15, we turn our attention to the process by which strategy is, and should be, formulated and implemented. Remembering that our focus throughout is on strategic thinking rather than formal strategic planning, we discuss the relationship between the concepts and approach advocated in this book and sensible strategic planning processes in firms.

CHAPTER 2

BUSINESS STRATEGY

2.1 INTRODUCTION

The core of strategic management as a practical endeavor is formulating a successful strategy for the firm. In Chapter 1, we asserted that strategic thinking is about understanding the relationships among the firm's internal and external contexts, its actions and its performance (as illustrated in Figure 1-2 and reproduced here as Figure 2-1). In this chapter, we describe how a manager who has a mental map of these relationships can define a strategy that acts as a guide to decision making for all members of the organization. To make the concept of strategy more concrete, we begin by describing the components a strategy should have. We also want to distinguish strategy from other terms that are related to it, such as vision, mission, values, and purpose. These are useful complements to strategy, but they are generally different from and imperfect substitutes for it.

Having described what we mean by strategy, we will discuss how to identify a strategy in practice and then how to evaluate it. We round out the chapter by outlining the steps beyond strategy identification and evaluation that a business unit typically goes through when it tries to change its strategy. Since the goal of subsequent chapters is to provide the building blocks for developing and implementing a strategy, we need to know the steps involved in doing that before we proceed.

2.2 DESCRIBING BUSINESS STRATEGY

To be a useful guide for decision making, a strategy must have elements that clearly define the firm's goals and the direction it will take to achieve them. Although there are many ways a manager might choose to accomplish this, any coherent strategy should have four components. First, it should include a clear set of long-term goals. Second, it should define the scope of the firm, the kinds of products the firm will offer, the markets it will pursue, and the broad areas of activity it will undertake. Third, a strategy should have a clear statement of what competitive advantage it will achieve and sustain. Finally, the strategy must present the essential logic that is suggested in Figure 2-1; what is it about the firm's internal context that will allow it to achieve a competitive advantage in

20 CHAPTER 2 • BUSINESS STRATEGY

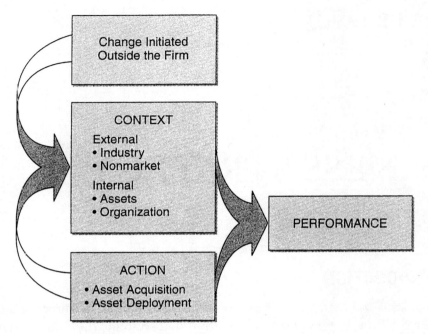

FIGURE 2-1 Dynamics of Business Strategy

the environment in which it has chosen to compete? We will define each of these components and describe how the final component, logic, ties them together.

Goals

The first element of a coherent strategy is a clear set of long-term goals toward which strategy is directed. These long-term goals typically refer to the market position or status that the firm hopes to achieve through its strategy. For example, long-term goals might be to "dominate the market," to be "the technology leader," or to be "the premium quality firm." By "long term" we mean that these goals are enduring. They are different from the specific targets that a firm might set for a particular planning period. A long-term goal, such as having the highest quality products in the industry, is not one that can be achieved and then checked off a list. Rather, it is a goal that may take a long time to attain and once achieved, it must be actively maintained.

By including long-term goals within the strategy, we may seem to be confusing ends (long-term goals) with means (strategy). But the two are closely intertwined. "Market dominance" is a goal because it states what the firm hopes to achieve. Yet it is also part of the strategy because it has implications for the plan of action the firm should pursue. A strategy designed to support market dominance will usually imply a different set of activities from a strategy intended to support being one of many equal competitors. Being the "lowest price" producer, for example, is consistent with market dominance. Setting a price that matches competitors' prices is more likely to be consistent with a strategy of sharing the market.

The goals should be clearly directional. Goals can be thought of as the "where" of the strategy: Where do the managers of the firm want it to be? To be directional, goals must be more specific than the overarching edict of "maximize profit." A long-term goal like profit-maximization is too broad to have much strategic content. In some circumstances, dominating the market might maximize a firm's profits; in others, a firm will maximize its profit by being a niche player in an industry dominated by another firm. In sum, long-term goals should provide guidance for what actions the firm should take.

Beyond the primary purpose of helping to explicate the strategy, incorporating goals within it can serve at least two other purposes. The first is motivational. Providing a common target can give employees a sense of purpose as well as the knowledge that they and their fellow workers are working towards a common goal. The second is competitive. By clearly staking out a desired competitive position, the firm may be able to persuade rivals to focus their efforts elsewhere. For example, GE's commitment to being "number one or two" in the markets it serves is not lost on its competitors!

Scope

The scope of a business defines the activities in which it will engage. This includes a definition of the products, markets, geographies, technologies, and processes with which it will be involved. The scope nearly always defines the products and services the firm will provide and the markets (demographic, sectoral, or geographic) it targets. An online retailer of baby products, for example, might define its scope as advice and products for expectant and new mothers in the United States. It may also define which of the activities in the value chain for these products and services it will do in-house. Will development of the Web site be conducted in-house to ensure the desired interface or outsourced to a Web development specialist that can reduce cost by achieving economies of scale? As we shall see, for some companies the scope may also include a definition of what technological capabilities the firm intends to master. Scope is the "what" of the strategy: *What* kinds of products will the firm produce, *what* activities will it carry out in-house, and *what* markets will it target?

The scope also defines (implicitly) the activities the firm will *not* undertake. Much of the bite of the strategy comes from this feature. Companies are bombarded with opportunities to venture out of their current scope of activities and with arguments from line managers about the merits of bringing currently outsourced activities in-house. Some business advisors argue that firms will be better off if they sharply focus their activity, while others emphasize the importance of expanding the firm's scope to embrace new opportunities. The statement of scope defines the firm's position with respect to these broad and controversial strategic issues. The scope of the firm's strategy minimizes time-consuming confusion about what activities the firm should pursue and allows it to focus on performing well within that scope.

Competitive Advantage

Competitive advantage is the "how" of strategy. It defines *how* the firm intends to achieve its long-term goals within its chosen scope. Since the firm faces actual or potential competitors, it must have a compelling reason to expect that it will be able to compete effectively against them. As the phrase "competitive advantage" suggests, a high-performance firm must achieve advantage over its competitors. To be successful, a firm does not need to have an advantage over *all* of its competitors. Many markets have room for several firms that have parity in their ability to compete. Generally speaking, however, a firm will do better if its source of competitive advantage is unique.

There is great variety in the potential sources of competitive advantage. These include lower manufacturing costs than one's competitors, higher quality products, greater customer loyalty, the capacity to innovate more quickly, a superior service capability, a better business location, an information technology system that enables the firm to replenish inventory more quickly and efficiently than rivals, and so on. While the list is long, most forms of competitive advantage mean either that a firm can produce some service or product that its customers value more than those produced by competitors or that it can produce its service or product at a lower cost than its competitors.

A firm that is better at something than most of its actual or potential competitors has an advantage in that activity. But this can be a *competitive* advantage only if being better at that activity contributes to the firm's ability to meet its long-term goals. A firm that is best in its industry at filing documents has an advantage in document filing. This will not provide it a competitive advantage, however, unless document filing speed is somehow linked to the basis on which firms compete. For a hospital, document filing speed might be related to service quality; the more rapidly patient records are re-filed, the more likely they will be available the next time the patient comes in for treatment. For a mining company, it is hard to imagine that the speed at which it files its documents will have much effect on its ability to compete effectively.

Logic

Perhaps the most important element of a strategy is the logic by which the firm intends to achieve its goals. To see why, consider the following (simplistic) example:

> Our strategy is to dominate the U.S. market for inexpensive coffee mugs by being the low-cost, mass-market producer.

This strategy contains a long-term goal and a simple description of both scope and competitive advantage. The goal is to dominate the coffee mug market. The scope is to produce inexpensive mugs for the U.S. mass market. The competitive advantage is the firm's low cost. Yet the example omits a crucial element of any strategy: an explanation of why this strategy will work. Why will this product scope and this competitive advantage result in high performance for this particular firm in this particular industry? The "why" is the logic of the strategy.

To see what logic contributes to a strategy, consider the following expanded strategy:

Our strategy is to dominate the U.S. market for inexpensive coffee mugs by being the low-priced manufacturer selling through mass-market channels. Our low price in these channels will generate high volume and, because there are economies of scale in the production of mugs, will make us the low-cost producer enabling us to achieve favorable margins even with a low price.

This more complete strategy does two things. First, it answers the "why" question. In particular, it explains the linkage among the "low cost," the "low prices," and the goal of "dominating the market." Low costs enable the firm to charge low prices, which generate large volumes. Economies of scale in production imply that the large volumes enable the firm to produce at low costs. If the firm has the largest market share (which it will if it "dominates the market") and if economies of scale persist at these very large volumes, the firm has a competitive advantage over its rivals. This is what enables it to charge lower prices than its competitors. Figure 2-2 represents the mutually reinforcing elements of this logic.

Second, the more complete strategy makes explicit some of the assumptions about the firm and its environment that must be true if the strategy is to succeed. For example, it must be true that economies of scale are sufficient to give the firm the cost advantage it believes it will have over smaller competitors.

Obviously, even this "more complete" strategy is a simplified example. In practice, the firm's strategic goals are often more complex, its scope is more detailed, its sources of competitive advantage are more numerous and specific, and its logic is more intricate. Our purpose here has been to describe the components of a strategy rather than to provide a complete or realistic one. Later in the chapter, we provide a more richly textured example. More important than the details and specificity, however, is the idea of what the logic does: the notion that *the logic contains the core argument for why the firm will succeed.* Until one is able to articulate how the goals, scope, and competitive advantage come together to provide a coherent and convincing case for firm success, you have only a list of elements, not a strategy.

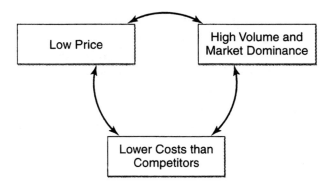

FIGURE 2-2 The Logic of the More Complete Strategy

2.3 RELATIONSHIP OF STRATEGY TO MISSION, PURPOSE, VALUES, AND VISION

The purpose of strategy is to guide the decisions the firm makes, but it is not the only guide that firms use. The choices they make are also affected by the values endorsed by the firm, the vision embraced by its leaders, and the mission it pursues. Indeed, words such as "values," "mission," "purpose," and "vision" are often used interchangeably with "strategy." In our view, values, vision, and mission are often complements to a strategy, but they also serve distinct purposes and should not be confused with strategy.

Mission, Purpose, and Values

Firms often commit their major goals and corporate philosophy to writing in a Mission Statement or a Statement of Purpose. Though varied in its structure and form, the statement typically describes the firm's *raison d'etre*, its reason for existing.[1] It also sometimes outlines the "core values" on which the company is based and to which it expects corporate behavior to conform. The statement of Sunrise Medical reproduced in Figure 2-3 is an example of the kind of statement we have in mind. This company (which uses the term "charter" for "scope") prominently posts its statement in its annual reports and on its Web page. The way in which it emphasizes the statement suggests that its managers believe it is important.

The mission or purpose parts of these statements seldom contain the essential elements of a strategy. In particular, although they sometimes define product scope and may refer to competitive advantage, they almost never clearly state the logic supporting the firm's strategy. The Sunrise statement is more detailed than many. It informs the reader that the firm produces rehabilitation aids, and it suggests that product superiority is a potential competitive advantage for Sunrise. Other statements lack even these rudimentary clues to a firm's strategy. Consider, for example, the mission statement in Figure 2-4.

This statement clearly fails what might be referred to as the "person on the bus test." If a person on a bus read it without the company name attached to it, he or she would have little hope of identifying the company, much less of discerning what its strategy might be. The scope of the company is almost a complete mystery. (Is this a TV station? the Disney Corporation?) Moreover, while (1) and (2) list some purported sources of competitive advantage, they are short on specifics (How, for example, will the company "understand the entertainment interests of the consumer better than anyone else"?), and the logic is not explained. Told that this is the Mission Statement of the Blockbuster Entertainment Group (a division of Viacom Inc.) that operates a chain of video rental stores, the bus rider might wonder how Blockbuster will deliver "unique products."

---

[1] See Jeffrey Abrahams, *The Mission Statement Book* (Berkeley, CA: Ten Speed Press, 1995), for a number of examples.

RELATIONSHIP OF STRATEGY TO MISSION, PURPOSE, VALUES, AND VISION

> **Sunrise Charter:** Sunrise Medical designs, manufactures and markets products used in institutional and homecare settings that address the recovery, rehabilitation and respiratory needs of the patient.
>
> **Sunrise Mission:** To improve people's lives by creating innovative, high quality products.
>
> **Sunrise Values:**
>
> 1. *Product Superiority:* We are a product-driven company: We are only as good as the products we make. We are committed as a corporation to offering products with genuine superiority in quality, innovation and value, but the most important of these is quality. Our quality standard is: do it right the first time.
> 2. *Service to Customers:* In our company, the customer comes first. Our customer service goal is to Exceed Customer Expectations Every Day: EXCEED. We must outperform our competitors in demonstrating sensitivity and responsiveness to our customers' needs.
> 3. *Respect for Associates:* We value the diversity of our Associates and believe in the dignity and worth of every individual. We will treat our Associates with fairness and respect, while empowering them to think independently and act resourcefully. Every job is important and must be performed well if we are to succeed. Our company provides equal opportunity worldwide for all Associates to achieve personal growth and fulfillment in their careers.
> 4. *Teamwork:* All of us together are stronger and wiser than any of us is individually. We will foster within our company the attitude of a championship team: a spirit of enthusiasm, dedication and fun while working together in the pursuit of common goals. We will be known as people who care about our customers, our products, our company and one another.
> 5. *Performance:* We must earn an attractive return for our stockholders, which in turn ensures our corporate future and permits us to reinvest in growth. The key to corporate performance is achieving continuous improvement in every area of our business. To do this we must develop our core competencies, operate with the latest methods and technologies, and invest in education to improve our critical skills.
> 6. *Social Responsibility:* Through our commitment to corporate excellence, we will improve the welfare of those who use our products and advance the progress of society. We will respect and help protect the environment. We will also be good citizens of every community and every country in which we operate, thereby contributing to global prosperity and harmony.
> 7. *Integrity:* We are committed as an organization to acting with integrity and character. When faced with moral choices, we will do the right thing. We will bring professionalism and proper business conduct to everything we do. Above all, we are dedicated to being a company with integrity.

FIGURE 2-3 Charter, Mission, and Values Statement of Sunrise Medical

The statement of company values is usually even less like a strategy. Some are simply a list of unexceptional virtues (**integrity, customer service, treating employees well, and so forth**). These routine **lists include many statements that could not reason**ably be contradicted. Could a **firm, for example, state that it believes in treating** employees badly or in providing **shoddy service?** Other statements have less routine

> "[Our] mission is to be the best provider of entertainment options that meet consumer needs. We will accomplish this by:
>
> 1. Understanding the entertainment interests of the consumer better than anyone else.
> 2. Delivering unique products with the highest level of customer service.
>
> Our resolve to consistently provide the best customer entertainment experience will result in exciting opportunities for our employees and an exceptional return for our investors."

FIGURE 2-4 A Mission Statement

content. The statement from Sunrise Medical, for example, contains a paragraph on "social responsibility" that, if adhered to, might distinguish Sunrise from its competitors. Even when the value statement has substance, it usually has little in common with what we have called strategy. Consider, for example, the values statement of a leading company listed in Figure 2-5. Which company's values are these? Apart from the hint provided by the word "technology," you would be hard-pressed to guess which of many thousands of companies that might aspire to these values actually produced this statement.[2]

If they have little strategic value, why do firms formulate and publicize these kinds of statements? A cynical view is that they are largely public relations statements; indeed, the wide publicity given to them seems to indicate that managers believe they will enhance the firm's image. But in fact, mission and values statements can serve several positive functions:

- First, the mission statement can clarify the firm's goals, reducing the tendency for people to work at cross-purposes. Some strategic management scholars, for example, stress the importance of consistency between the views of the company's leaders and the company's strategy. A mission statement may help promote this congruence.
- Second, in not-for-profit organizations, the mission statement can serve to inform the organizations' external constituency (including potential donors) about the overarching goals of the organization. Because not-for-profit organizations tend to have more varied overarching goals than for-profits, this kind of statement may be critical to defining the organization's goals.
- Third, to the extent that the firm can commit itself to a distinctive set of values, these may have positive effects on suppliers, customers, and employees. The device that enables the firm to commit to these values is its reputation. We will return to the role of values and reputation later in this book.

Our main point, however, is that whatever merit these statements have, they should not be confused with a statement of the firm's strategy.

[2] In fact, this is the values statement of Applied Materials, a leading producer of semiconductor manufacturing equipment (Abrahams, *The Mission Statement Book*, p. 97).

> *Close to Customer*
> More than technology, customers define our accomplishments.
> *Achievement Oriented*
> Aggressive goals and meeting commitments drive our success.
> *Respect for the Individual*
> Mutual trust and respect are shared by all.
> *Honesty and Integrity*
> Honesty and integrity are essential for building trust.
> *Teamwork*
> Effectiveness increases when we exchange ideas and share responsibilities.
> *Performance and Rewards*
> Commitment and performance ensure growth.
> *Professional Management*
> Professional managers lead employees to translate values into action.
> *Excellence and Quality*
> Every task can be continually improved.
> *Global Awareness*
> Embracing different perspectives leads to a wealth of opportunities.
> *Obligations to Stockholders*
> Return long-term value to our investors.
> *Positive Social Contribution*
> Make a meaningful contribution in our communities.

FIGURE 2-5 A Statement of Values

Vision

To develop a strategy with a coherent internal logic, the strategist needs to understand where the firm and the industry are headed. The general manager must have some sense about technological trajectories, competitors' likely actions, and developing market opportunities. Because these cannot be precisely and definitively described, the manager has to make some assumptions about them, about the way they interact, and about what outcomes are likely. Forecasting how this related set of events will unfold requires foresight because the current situation often provides few hints about what the future holds. Because of the foresight that is required to imagine how events might unfold and the role the firm might play in shaping that future to the firm's advantage, the term "vision" is often used to describe the strategist's plan for closing the gap between current reality and a potential future. For example, Bennis and Nanus describe the role of vision as follows:

> To choose a direction, a leader must first have developed a mental image of a possible and desirable future state of the organization ... which we call a *vision*. [A] vision articulates a view of a realistic, credible, attractive future for the organization. ... With a vision, the leader provides the all-important bridge from the present to the future of the organization.[3]

[3] Warren Bennis and Burt Nanus, *Leaders: The Strategies for Taking Charge* (New York: Harper and Row, 1985).

Having a vision of the future might (and often does) contribute to formulating a good strategy and motivating the firm's employees to achieve it. Indeed, as we saw, it is difficult to articulate a strategy without also indicating the long-term goals at which it is aimed.

Developing and communicating an envisioned future for a firm in a rapidly changing and uncertain world is a leadership function of general managers. The strategist's, and even the firm's, value added can sometimes depend on the creativity and innovation of the vision. Especially for a new organization or a firm involved in fundamentally changing its strategic direction, a clear (and clearly articulated) vision of where the strategy is intended to take the company and why it has a chance for success is important to attract and motivate employees and investors. Managers themselves believe that vision is a key role of senior management. For example, one survey indicates that 98 percent of international senior managers believe that conveying a strong sense of vision is the most important role for a CEO, and that strategy formulation to achieve a vision is the CEO's most important skill.[4]

At the same time, a vision is not always necessary for strategy, and, more importantly, it is never sufficient. Some very boring strategies that require little creativity to formulate are successful. Particularly in industries in which change is slow and incremental, a successful strategy may require little vision. Conversely, a great vision without a supporting strategy is unlikely to succeed. Hundreds of companies have been built on the founder's vision of how consumers would use the Internet, and most have failed. Some have failed because the vision was wrong. Others have failed because they had no strategy enabling them to succeed. There was no strategy to guide the firm in its acquisition and deployment of assets that would provide it with competitive advantage *given* the vision. At its best, vision can guide the formulation of strategy, but it is not a substitute for it.

2.4 THE STRATEGY STATEMENT

Even when a firm is pursuing a clear, logical strategy, the firm may never have publicly articulated it. Typically, the company's annual report and its other public disclosures describe some elements of the strategy. In the United States, for example, a publicly held firm's annual report and its other filings with the Securities and Exchange Commission usually say something about the scope of the firm and its competitive advantage. However, those documents generally do not lay out long-term goals (except perhaps in a vague and not strategically meaningful way), and, more importantly, they do not explain how the firm intends to tie the pieces together to outperform its competition. The absence of a public, explicit strategy statement is in sharp contrast to the mission statement, which the firm often takes pains to disseminate widely. The reason for this difference is, of course, that the firm often wishes to keep its strategic intentions hidden from its rivals, whereas the mission statement is intended to communi-

---

[4] Results of Korn/Ferry International survey as quoted in Joseph Quigley, *Vision: How Leaders Develop It, Share It, and Sustain It* (New York: McGraw-Hill, 1993).

cate core values, purpose, and mission to employees, investors, suppliers, customers, and the general public.

While it is understandable that a firm would refrain from publishing its strategy, some firms do not even explicitly articulate their strategy *privately*. Perhaps the most common reason for not articulating a strategy is that the senior general managers have a mutual understanding of what the strategy is and need not bother to formulate an explicit strategy statement.

A second reason is that the firm may be pursuing its strategy un-self-consciously. That is, it may be operating within a clear scope and successfully outperforming its rivals with a clear source of competitive advantage without ever having analyzed why it is successful or what the logic of its actions and policies might be. Whether the firm originally embarked on its strategy by following a grand design or stumbled on it through a process of incremental change or pure chance, the key to its competitive advantage may long ago have become embodied in its routines, policies, and organizational structure.

Once a firm has hit (or stumbled) on a recipe for success, it can replicate its success without even analyzing why it is successful, provided its environment does not change. In such an organization, each part plays its role as shaped by the firm's history. When individuals within those roles leave, others who continue that function replace them. The various parts work together, like a well-oiled machine, similarly ignorant of how the pieces fit together or how the whole functions. In such cases it is sometimes easier for an outsider to divine what the firm's strategy actually is than it is for an insider who is blinded or biased by the idiosyncratic nature of the role he or she performs.

The third reason for a firm not to have an explicit, articulated strategy is that the firm is confused about its strategy or has a strategy that has no compelling logic. Since the process of precisely articulating the strategy reveals these inconsistencies, often accompanied by disagreement and conflict among senior management, such firms often prefer to focus on the details of the next year's business plan rather than to confront the fundamentals of their strategy.

Benefits of an Explicit Strategy Statement

Firms can sometimes function well without an explicit strategy statement, but it is generally good practice to be explicit about the strategy. Articulating and communicating to the relevant decision makers a strategy for the business have several benefits:

- *Clarity:* Even if all senior managers believe they know the strategy, the failure to write it down allows for ambiguity that can lead to lack of focus. Moreover, even if the senior management does have a consensus about the strategy, differences in how it is articulated to those who must implement it often lead to unnecessary confusion and conflict. Strategy can be a framework for choosing actions only if those who make the choices know what the strategy is.

- *Coordination:* If the strategy is explicit and well-communicated, people throughout the organization can "pull" in the same direction without having to check constantly that their actions are coordinated with each other. That is, an explicit strategy is a coordinating mechanism. This can also occur with an implicit strategy that the entire organization understands, but creating a common understanding is easier when the strategy is made explicit.

- *Incentives:* If an organization can commit to a specific strategy, employees will have some assurance that the activities the organization values today are the same ones it will value in the future. Therefore, to the extent that rewards for today's effort depend on the fruits of that effort tomorrow, it is easier to provide incentives for that effort. Aguilar expresses this view as follows:

  > Consistency of word and deed on the leader's part is absolutely necessary if others are to commit themselves to the personal and business risks associated with new and unproven courses of action. The general manager who runs hot and cold will fail to encourage confidence in others ... Nobody wants to go out on a limb and risk being abandoned at the first sound of cracking wood."[5]

- *Efficiency:* Day-to-day decisions can be evaluated in terms of whether they "fit" the existing strategy. This is considerably less expensive in terms of management time than doing a full-scale evaluation of the merits of all possibilities.

- *Evaluation/Adaptation:* It is usually possible to articulate the performance goals the firm should achieve from following the stated strategy. This is useful in tracking how well the strategy is performing. Having an explicit strategy based on clearly understood assumptions may also make it easier to change the strategy when circumstances require change.

- *Change:* A significant change in the firm's strategy almost always requires a clear articulation of the proposed new strategy, so that all relevant parts of the firm can implement it.

These benefits of being explicit about strategy must be weighed against some potentially adverse effects. The most important of these effects is that being explicit about the strategy can reinforce rigidity and inertia. Even worthwhile experimentation beyond the boundaries of the current strategy may be blocked by middle managers on the grounds that it falls outside the current strategy. The issue of balancing focus on the current strategy with exploration into new areas is taken up in Chapter 5 and discussed more fully in Chapter 15. In most circumstances, however, we believe that the benefits of being explicit about strategy far outweigh any potential costs.

The Form and Use of the Strategy Statement

When a firm decides to be explicit about its strategy, we call the vehicle that the firm uses to describe its strategy a "strategy statement." Earlier we gave an example of a

---

[5] Francis Aguilar, *General Managers in Action* (New York: Oxford University Press, 1985), p. 71.

complete one-sentence statement of strategy. Most firms will not be able to boil their strategy down to a single sentence. The long-term goals, scope, and sources of competitive advantage may each involve a number of points, and the logic that binds them may take several paragraphs to explain. The statement needs to be detailed enough to do justice to its components; yet it must be concise enough to be succinctly communicated. Most people who have experience with attempting to communicate strategy stress the need for simplicity and brevity. Think of the strategy statement as an "elevator pitch": a statement of the firm's strategy that is sufficiently detailed to be useful to the functional managers who must implement the strategy, yet concise enough to be delivered in an elevator ride.

An Example: Borders Books

We present a strategy statement for Borders, Inc., a book distributor employing a superstore format.[6] Borders distributes both through its traditional offline "bricks and mortar" stores and through a newer online division, Borders.com. In Figure 2-6 we have presented the strategy for Borders before its adoption of online distribution. We have done this both to focus on a somewhat simpler strategy, but also to show later in the chapter how Borders should think about adapting to external change with the advent of online bookstores.

Note, first, that the entire statement is only about a page long. Note, too, that while the strategy statement may change a little in its details over time, this basic strategy is likely to be enduring. In particular, the long-term goals will take some time to achieve and will take significant effort to maintain once they have been achieved. The scope is clear about which activities in the value chain the firm will provide itself and which it will not. Finally, observe that while the purported sources of competitive advantage are outlined, the competitive advantages themselves are vacuous without a statement of the logic that ties those competitive advantages to the company's goals and scope.

This strategy statement illustrates several of the advantages of being explicit about strategy that we discussed above. First, clarity about the scope of the strategy can help to focus management's efforts on growth by emphasizing the kinds of stores and geographic areas that the firm has chosen for expansion. Second, the logic of the strategy makes it clear that the firm ought to be interested in cost-saving innovations that will enable it to reduce unit costs while maintaining or increasing service levels. Understanding the logic of the firm's strategy will provide employees with the right incentives to suggest improvements that advance the logic of the business. Third, the in-store employees are a key part of the strategy as outlined in this statement. Helping them to see the important role they play in the company's strategy may also motivate them.

---

[6] Since the details of firms' strategies are typically highly confidential, the strategy statement in Figure 2-6 has been inferred by the authors from publicly available information. The example is meant only to be illustrative of the components of a strategy statement, rather than a description of Borders' actual strategy.

BORDERS' STRATEGY STATEMENT

Long-term goals: Borders will be the leading retail distribution outlet for books in the United States measured by the number of books sold and revenue market share. We will have the greatest revenue per square foot of any book retailer and the highest margin per book. Our customers will have the most satisfying book purchasing experience in terms of variety of books offered, in-store availability of desired titles, and helpfulness of staff. We will expand from our base in the United States to Australia, New Zealand, Singapore and the United Kingdom.

Scope: Borders will run a chain of large (in excess of 20,000-sq. ft.) bookstores carrying a wide variety of titles (in excess of 80,000) in each store. We will be located in all major metropolitan areas in the United States and Canada. Our facilities will be leased rather than purchased, and, while designed to fit into the local architecture, they will share a common layout and common information systems. Most stores will have a coffee bar, the operation of which will be outsourced. We have developed and continue to maintain and improve a proprietary information technology system for tracking and managing inventory. We are not vertically integrated into the production of books.

Competitive Advantages: We believe that the following are key sources of competitive advantage:

- Our large scale
- Our proprietary inventory system
- Our highly trained in-store staff
- Customer awareness of our name and reputation for service and value
- Our prime locations of existing stores
- Perception of our stores among real estate developers as valuable "anchor tenants."

Logic: Our wide variety of titles, low prices, highly trained staff, and attractive stores provide an attractive shopping experience for our customers, making us their first choice in bookstores. The high volumes this generates in each store coupled with the size of the chain give us significant purchasing power that enables us to procure books at favorable prices. Furthermore, our proprietary inventory management gives us superior knowledge of what to stock and minimizes "out of stock" occurrences, optimizes inventory on hand, and minimizes returns of books to suppliers. Our unit costs are therefore the lowest in the industry, allowing us to have the highest margins despite having below average prices. While we have significant expenses in terms of creating and maintaining our proprietary information systems, training, brand advertising, and administration, our ability to spread those expenses over many stores enables us to keep our operating expenses a low fraction of revenue. Our current store locations give us a first-mover location advantage, and our reputation for attracting traffic makes us an attractive anchor tenant in new locations, facilitating growth through new stores, allowing us to leverage our competitive advantages into new locations.

FIGURE 2-6 Strategy Statement for Borders, Inc.

2.5 DEVELOPING STRATEGY: THE STRATEGY PROCESS

So far we have discussed what a strategy should do and what components it should have. In the rest of this chapter, we offer some comments on the process of developing a strategy. Formulating a strategy that is an effective guide to action is both an art that individual managers must develop and a process that a well-managed firm must implement. The individual manager must first have the tools she or he needs to analyze the firm's internal and external context. Much of this text is devoted to providing the essential tools. She or he must also understand what role strategy plays within the firm and the elements that a strategy should contain. This has been the topic of this chapter.

It is also important, however, to recognize that strategy is developed within a firm. The final product will necessarily be shaped by the history of that firm, the processes it has in place for making fundamental business decisions, and the interests and perspectives of its senior managers. Typically, these factors come together in a "strategy process," a (sometimes formal) process through which strategy is defined and evaluated by the firm's managers. The issue of strategy process will be discussed in the final chapter of this book, but we want to complete our current discussion by sketching the major steps such a process might involve. The conceptual steps are illustrated in Figure 2-7.

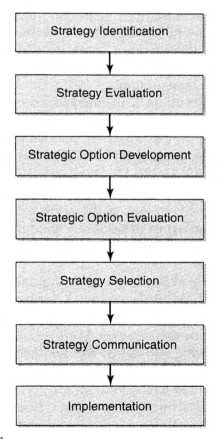

FIGURE 2-7 Steps in Setting Strategy

For our current purpose, the steps of strategy identification and evaluation are most relevant, and we will focus on them. The remaining steps are particularly important when the firm is changing its strategy or, in the case of a new firm, establishing an initial strategy.

Strategy Identification

It might seem strange to start with the notion that the manager needs to identify the firm's strategy. After all, it may seem obvious that he or she will know what the strategy is. However, this is not always the case. Previously, we described a firm for which strategy is embodied in its routines but has never been articulated. Managers at this type of firm who want to develop a strategy statement will first have to "reverse engineer" the firm's routines. They will have to look at what the firm does and try to figure out what strategy might be consistent with that set of activities. Managers also have to identify the firm's strategy when some of the firm's actions have diverged from its formal strategy. If, for example, the firm's external environment has changed significantly, the managers may have responded by taking appropriate actions. If these actions are inconsistent with the old strategy, the strategy has *de facto* been changed, perhaps without the managers' recognition of how it has changed. Over time, small changes can cumulate to produce a *de facto* strategy that bears little resemblance to the official strategy. In these circumstances, identifying the existing strategy is necessary to crafting an accurate and useful strategy statement. But creating a strategy statement is not the only reason for identifying a firm's strategy. Identifying a firm's current strategy is also the starting point for the general managers responsible for developing and overseeing strategy implementation.

Outsiders who are analyzing the firm either for competitive or investment reasons or with an eye to a merger or acquisition also want to identify the firm's strategy. For them, it is tempting simply to examine what the firm may have said its strategy is. Such statements can often be found in its financial reports, annual reports, Web pages, investor information kits, and so on. However, as we have noted above, such statements are rarely coherent and comprehensive articulations of strategy. To understand a firm's strategy, one also needs to look at the firm's actual policies and what the firm actually does: that is, its pattern of decisions. Sometimes what the firm claims as its strategy is in conflict with what the firm does. More often, what the firm does provides additional information about its strategy.

To return to the example of Borders, a key component of its strategy is to provide superior customer service. If this is the reality of Borders' strategy rather than wishful thinking on its part, we would expect it to have a set of human resources management policies that are aligned with this strategy. We would look for personnel recruiting and selection policies, training programs, and compensation schemes that are well suited to developing a workforce that delivers high-quality customer service.

Thus the starting point for strategy identification is an examination of the firm's approach to business in each of its key areas of operation: finance, sales and marketing, manufacturing, procurement, R&D, marketing, distribution, product line, pricing, formal and informal organization structure, human resources management policies, and so on. From an examination of the firm's practices in each of these areas, we can generally determine the key elements of the scope of the strategy as well as the areas in which the firm might have competitive advantage. The final step is to attempt to infer what logic ties the pieces together. That is basically an inductive exercise in which one attempts to build a coherent argument for how the firm's actions and policies combine to form a cohesive strategy. As we discuss in the following section, it is easiest to infer the logic of the strategy when the strategy is in fact compelling. When what the firm is doing doesn't make much sense, there may be no logic to infer.

Strategy Evaluation: Testing the Logic

Logic is the component of strategy that brings the other elements together. The logic of the strategy contains the argument for how the scope and competitive advantage identified in the strategy will enable the firm to reach its goals given its internal assets and its external environment. Strategy evaluation is testing whether that logic is compelling.

To evaluate the logic, the managers want to ask: "What must be true about this firm and about the environment in which we compete if this strategy is to be successful?" If the strategy calls for the firm to offer the most advanced products, the managers want to ask whether the firm's internal context has the strategic assets it needs to produce more advanced products than its competitors and whether its buyers want more advanced products enough to pay the cost of developing them. Or, to return to our one-sentence example on page 23, a strategy might depend on costs declining with output. If the firm's technology has only negligible economies of scale, the logic of the strategy is flawed. It might be true that a low-cost position would be advantageous given the firm's external environment, but the firm's internal context—its technology in this case—is inconsistent with achieving a low-cost position.

Because testing the logic requires looking at both the firm's internal and external environments, practitioners commonly speak of "opportunity analysis" and "asset analysis." An opportunity analysis looks at whether there is, in fact, an attractive opportunity in the external context that this strategy can exploit. Does the world really want a better mousetrap? An asset analysis examines the firm's internal context: Does this firm have the human and physical capital necessary to build a better mousetrap, and are those assets organized in a way that allows the firm to be better than its competitors at building mousetraps? Although it is convenient to separate the analysis this way, it is important to remember that the pieces all have to fit together for the logic to work.

Our description of strategy evaluation has some common language with a tool known as *SWOT Analysis,* an acronym for the firm's *S*trengths, *W*eaknesses, *O*pportunities, and *T*hreats. SWOT Analysis encourages managers to identify the firm's strengths and weaknesses. The strengths and weaknesses component is similar to our asset analysis, and the threats and opportunities component is similar to our opportunities analysis. However, there are some key differences between the SWOT approach and a test of strategic logic. An application of the SWOT framework will produce an organized inventory of factors that are potentially relevant to the firm's strategic situation. This, however, is not enough. A firm's assets and opportunities must be appraised in terms of its strategy.

Suppose, for example, that we were to determine that Borders was weak in its financial controls and in understanding wide-area networking technology. Its weakness in financial controls might be of some concern, but since networking is critical to the proprietary inventory system on which its strategy depends, its networking weakness has much larger strategic significance. The threats and opportunities facing the firm must also be assessed in terms of its strategy. A book superstore must evaluate the opportunity to augment its scope by offering music CDs within its superstores versus, say, the chance to open small bookstores in addition to large superstores, in terms of how each possibility fits with the overall logic of its strategy. What implications does adding CDs have for staff training or for the quality of the "shopping experience," both of which might be important parts of the firm's competitive advantage in its current strategy? What implications does adding small bookstores have for the cost structure of the firm, and how will these stores compete with the existing small, independent bookstores that already offer this business format? Because there may be demand for a CD superstore and for small bookstores, these options represent opportunities for the firm. But deciding which opportunities to pursue requires analyzing them with respect to the firm's strategy and, specifically, the logic of the strategy.

Strategy Process and Strategic Change

Our primary goals in this chapter were to define the concept of strategy, compare it to related concepts such as mission and vision, and describe how a strategy statement might capture the essence of a firm's strategy. We also described how to identify a business unit's strategy in practice and outlined the criteria used to evaluate the strategy once it has been identified. In the process, we also have begun to develop the steps that are typically involved in strategic change and that we discuss in greater detail later in the book. As illustrated in Figure 2-7, strategy identification and evaluation are the initial steps in formulating and implementing a new strategy. The remaining steps are:

- *Developing Strategic Options:* If the strategy evaluation reveals problems with the firm's current strategy, the next step is to determine what other strategic options the firm has. A strategic option should be a coherent, self-contained strategy with the four elements of long-term goals, scope, competitive advantage, and logic.
- *Evaluating the Strategic Options:* Evaluating the strategic options raises issues similar to those discussed in evaluating the current strategy. The chosen strategy should exploit opportunities presented by the external environment for which the firm's strategic assets are well suited. But one does not generally expect the firm's *current* organization and assets to be consistent with that option. If a strategic option represents a departure from the previous strategy, the firm's internal context will likely have to be changed. The issue in evaluating an option is whether the firm can make the required changes.

- *Selecting a Strategy:* With the options clearly laid out, the firm has to select among them. The temptation at this stage is to attempt to combine the bits and pieces of various options that are most appealing to the managers. This amalgamation is particularly appealing when the firm has many constituencies, each of which has a stake in some piece of its strategy. Marketing, for example, might resist reducing the number of products the firm offers even if the change will benefit the firm as a whole. Or the R&D group might resist a movement from leading-edge to consumer-friendly products even though there is little demand for the "technically superior" product. If, however, the options are carefully developed, combining their elements will produce an incoherent strategy that may be ill-suited to any possible environment. It is because the temptation to waffle or merge elements of disparate strategies is so strong that we include a separate step for *selecting* a strategy.

- *Communicating a Strategy:* If a strategy is to guide the firm's actions, its employees must understand what the strategy is. Because it is difficult to get even a simple message about the firm's strategy across to everyone in the organization, clarity and brevity are crucial. Moreover, managers with experience in communicating strategy stress the importance of repetition and retaining the same strategy statement unless the firm has indeed made a fundamental change in its strategy.

- *Implementing a Strategy:* Strategy implementation is the process of executing the strategy. From a process point of view, it is conceptually attractive to draw a bright line between formulation and implementation. First you decide what to do, and then you do it. However, the starting conditions for developing and evaluating strategy are formed by prior implementation actions. For example, formulating a new product strategy might be necessary only because implementing the current strategy resulted in a major product innovation. Similarly, the development of a culture of trust and respect may provide the basis for a high-quality service orientation that may be a potential source of competitive advantage later on. It is therefore misleading to think of implementation as merely the mechanical carrying out of a plan of action. There is a strong feedback loop from implementation to formulation.

To illustrate the kind of analysis required for the steps listed in Figure 2-7, let's go back to Borders at the time when online sales of books were just beginning. Strategy evaluation might reveal that the company's offline ("bricks and mortar") strategy is not well designed to counter the threat posed by retailing books over the Internet. The early success of Amazon.com is an example of the kind of contextual change that should trigger a full strategy reevaluation. This alternative channel reduces the demand for bookstore services and changes the kind of services potential customers value in book retailing. How do buyers make the tradeoff between ambiance—where Borders' stores have a purported advantage—and convenience which is Amazon.com's strength? What is the value of easy access to book reviews and customized recommendation lists that are provided on-line? How does this compare with the knowledge and helpfulness of Borders' sales staff? Answering these kinds of questions gives Borders a start on evaluating its current strategy given this new threat.

Once the nature of the external change is identified and the firm has some idea about how well its current strategy can respond to it, the firm can develop strategic options. One obvious option would be the one Borders has in fact pursued—to expand the scope of its strategy to include online retailing. To evaluate this option it would need to think about which of its assets could be leveraged in this endeavor and what assets it would need to acquire. For example, while it has some information technology know-how, it may need to acquire some Web development capabilities. It would also need to understand enough about online retailing to assess whether it could reasonably match Amazon.com's strengths and overcome any first-mover advantage Amazon.com might have. Borders might also need to expand its product line to include video and music to compete with the expanding product line at Amazon.com. Borders should also consider the history of losses at Amazon given its dominance of online book retailing. What will enable several competing firms to make a profit when Amazon.com could not when it had the market to itself?

To implement the online option, Borders must develop a clear strategy for that part of the business as a stand-alone venture as well as for the integrated business. For example, a potential competitive advantage that Borders has from having both an online presence and traditional stores is that it can arrange to handle returns of online purchases through the stores. Because the launch of the online operation represents a sharp strategic change for the company, the importance of clearly communicating this shift inside the company cannot be overestimated. Current employees need to know what changes they should make in their decision making and orientation. They also need to know that the company continues to support (if indeed it does) the prior strategy in its stores.

2.6 SUMMARY

In this chapter we have described the components of strategy as goals, competitive advantage, and logic. We have emphasized the logic component because it is the one so often overlooked. It is much easier to imagine some competitive advantage than to carefully describe how this firm has a distinctive ability to create that advantage and why this market environment will reward the "advantage" the firm can create. We have also tried to distinguish strategy from some commonly used and related approaches to directing the efforts of the firm, such as mission and vision, that typically do not have a logic. We have described the form of the strategy statement, discussed the benefits of having such a statement, and provided a detailed example of Borders books to illustrate what one should look like. Finally, we introduced the process by which strategy is formulated and implemented, focusing for now on the strategy identification and evaluation steps of the process. We return to the strategy process in greater detail in Chapter 15. We turn next to a more detailed exploration of competitive advantage.

CHAPTER 3

COMPETITIVE ADVANTAGE

3.1 INTRODUCTION

A firm achieves superior performance only if it can provide products or services that customers will pay more for than it costs the firm to provide them. That is, the firm must be able to *create value*. Value creation is at the heart of any successful strategy. However value creation is not enough. In order to prosper, the firm must also be able to *capture* the value it creates. In order to create *and* capture value the firm must have a sustainable competitive advantage.

We first describe why it is important to think about capturing value and not just about creating value. Then we discuss competitive advantage and what makes some competitive advantages transitory while others are enduring. Lastly, we develop an extended example of competitive advantage from product quality or low cost, and introduce the cost-quality frontier, a framework used throughout the book.

3.2 VALUE AND COMPETITIVE ADVANTAGE

Scholars of strategic management often stop with an analysis of value creation, simply advising firms to maximize the value they create. But that advice is inadequate because it assumes that an increase in value created will translate into an increase in profit. This need not be true. Indeed, a firm usually cannot retain all the value it generates. For example, competition may allow the firm's customers to capture some of the value the firm creates. The firm's employees may also capture some of that value. It is not unusual for a firm to substantially increase the value it creates without gaining a commensurate increase in profits. A famous example of this unhappy phenomenon is the invention of the CT (computed tomography) scanner.[1] EMI invented this technology

---

[1] Introduced by EMI in 1972, the CT scanner was initially used for brain scans. Innovations by EMI in 1974 alone are estimated to have added approximately $7 billion (1980 dollars) in value. EMI's profits from the technology were modest at best. See Manual Trajtenberg. *Economic Analysis of Product Innovation: The Case of CT Scanners* (Cambridge, MA: Harvard University Press, 1990).

and brought the first products to a market where demand was high. But EMI earned little of the tremendous value it created. While it initially dominated this market, EMI abandoned it seven years after it sold its first scanner. EMI found that it could not compete with firms like General Electric which rapidly copied the innovation and had the complementary resources for on-going product development, marketing, service, and distribution.

Sometimes a firm can capture value other firms create. In the CT scanner example, General Electric probably captured some of the value created by EMI. Or consider the case of America Online (AOL). Because of its premier status as the leading on-line content gateway, AOL has been able to capture much of the value generated by the content providers featured on its site.

To create and capture value consistently, there must be something special about the firm. Otherwise, a rival could replicate what the firm does, and the ensuing competition would sharply limit the firm's ability to capture value. The search for the underlying sources of such "specialness" is an obsession in strategic management; it is the field's version of the search for the Holy Grail. Every now and then a book appears with the claim that the author has found it, or at least its primary source, and a rush to exploit the fad *du jour* ensues. For example, recent candidates for the fundamental source of superior performance include quality, customer focus, and superior management of human resources. Firms have been told to redesign their business processes, get close to their customers, and empower their workers to enhance profitability.

The very notion that there could be a universal key to success is misguided: If the source of superior firm performance could so easily be identified and replicated, it would quickly cease to be a source of competitive advantage at all! Many firms create and capture value consistently, but the reasons for their success are extremely varied. It is not that customer focus, for example, is unimportant, but rather that there is no magic elixir good for all business problems. We believe instead that the way firms have been able to create and capture value varies because there is enormous heterogeneity among firms and industries. In this book we do not attempt to provide a checklist of universal keys to success or recipes for greatness. Instead, we examine how competitive advantage works in general. Our goal is to provide a method for assessing a firm's current competitive advantage, formulating a strategy to sustain it and creating additional advantage. We mention many specific forms of competitive advantages firms have developed, but our goal is to help managers understand competitive advantage.

We start from the position that any specific competitive advantage derives from the firm's context. By context we mean a firm's assets, its organization, its industry, and its nonmarket environment. As Figure 3-1 illustrates, competitive advantage is a characteristic of both the firm and its relationship to its environment. The firm has an asset—the ability to provide customer service efficiently, for example—and because that asset is superior to that of its competitors and is valued by its customers, it is a competitive advantage for the firm. Any such advantage the firm can exploit through its activity contributes to superior performance.

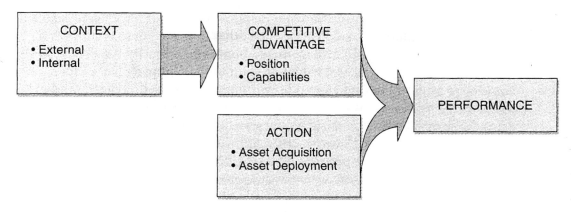

FIGURE 3-1 Sources of Competitive Advantage

3.3 TWO MAIN ROUTES TO COMPETITIVE ADVANTAGE

There are many kinds of competitive advantage, and they can be divided into two categories: advantages based on the firm's *position* and advantages based on the firm's *capabilities*.

To provide concrete examples of these kinds of competitive advantage, consider two hypothetical firms: Positions Inc. and Global Capabilities. They operate in different industries, but both earn returns on shareholders' equity that are well above average.

- *Positions Inc.* was founded in 1802 to provide a secure way to send cash over long distances. In the early days, a person wanting to send money deposited the funds (plus a healthy commission) at a nearby Position Inc. branch office. Positions Inc. would then send a message to its branch that was closest to the intended recipient of the money authorizing it to pay the sum deposited. Messages were initially sent by stagecoach, then by telegraph, and, ultimately, by a computer network. Although the communications technology has changed, Positions Inc. has never faced serious competition because potential rivals found setting up a competitive branch network prohibitively costly (especially because whenever they opened a branch, Positions Inc. mysteriously dropped the commission it charged in that location). Today, detractors describe Position Inc.'s computer system as "archaic," but managers at Positions Inc. say it works well enough. Customers sometimes complain about shoddy service (relative to, say, the local branch bank), but management responds that it is in the business of providing money transfer services, not entertainment.

- *Global Capabilities* is a Japanese firm that produces a broad range of consumer electronics products as a supplier for major electronics firms. Its customers, who themselves manufacture and sell electronic products, outsource the design and manufacture of selected products to Global Capabilities because Global can transform customer requirements into designs that are light, compact, and easy to manufacture. Its customers and rivals have long marveled at its competence in miniaturization and manufacturing, but have been unable to figure out how Global Capabilities can do what it does. There is some disagreement among Global's management about precisely why the firm is so adept. Certainly no single individual or team in the company has all the knowledge required to understand how it functions so well. Instead Global has complicated routines that bring together the expertise of its teams and coordinates the firm's activities. Outsiders observe how fluid and automatic this process appears to be, with each person knowing exactly whom to contact for help, when and how to participate, and when to hand off to someone else. A sophisticated, computerized project management system supports this human system, but other companies have had little success using similar information technology systems.

These (admittedly colorful) descriptions illustrate the two different kinds of competitive advantage and the futility of searching for the Holy Grail of unique and universal success factors. Whereas Global Capabilities takes prides in its world-class design capabilities and outstanding customer relations, Positions Inc. is weak in the former and atrocious in the latter. Positions Inc. enjoys a dominant position in its industry, but Global Capabilities has many rivals, including its primary customers.

Not only is Positions Inc. weak in customer relations, it does not appear to perform *any* particular function very well. Indeed, nothing about its internal context—neither its tangible and intangible assets nor how they are organized—is a source of strength for the company. For example, its information systems are central to the service it offers but are far from state of the art, and it has no proprietary know-how enabling it to distinguish its service from competitors Instead, the main source of Positions Inc.'s superior performance is that it was the first to enter the industry and build a network of branch offices. It yields extraordinary value to consumers because it provides the only way they can send money to almost anywhere from wherever they happen to be. No other firm has been able to duplicate Position Inc.'s pervasiveness. *Positions Inc.'s competitive advantage is its position as the dominant incumbent firm.* This position alone enables it to earn superior returns, even though it has no remarkable capabilities.

Compare its position to Global Capabilities'. *The essence of Global Capabilities' competitive advantage is its ability to miniaturize and its skill in design-for-manufacturing.* Nothing in its position distinguishes it from its rivals; it is not larger, it has no early-mover advantage, and it provides no valuable asset on which its performance depends. It has competitive advantage because Global is particularly good, indeed better than most of its competitors, at performing certain activities. Global earns its superior returns by exercising these capabilities over and over again for its customers. Since it would cost the customers more to perform these same functions themselves—if indeed they can do them themselves—or to outsource them to another firm, Global Capabilities earns a high return on its capabilities.

These two attributes of a firm and its relationship to its external environment—its *position* in its competitive environment and the *capabilities* that enable it to perform certain functions better than its rivals can—are the two main kinds of competitive advantage that firms can have. Each type of advantage can take a number of specific forms as we describe below, but a firm's competitive advantage can usually be traced to a positional or capability-based strength.

It is tempting to think of a capability as being primarily rooted in the firm's internal context and of position as being rooted primarily in the firm's external context. And indeed, this distinction has some bite. The analysis of positional advantage, for example, has been developed primarily by scholars focusing on the challenges and opportunities posed by the external environment. They tend to treat the firm's internal context as unimportant. From this perspective, the way for a firm to achieve superior performance is to find an advantageous and defensible position within its industry.

By contrast, scholars who primarily focus on the firm's internal context have been responsible for developing the analysis of capabilities-based advantage. They have explored ways the firm can acquire and organize tangible and intangible assets to outperform its competitors. From this perspective, a firm can achieve superior performance by exploiting the firm's assets and organizational structure and protecting them from imitation by rival firms. This view is discussed later in this chapter in the section on the "resource-based" view of the firm. The contributions made by scholars from the positional advantage school of thought are covered in Chapter 6.

Both sources of advantage, however, depend on the firm's internal *and* external context. A superior capability arises in the firm's internal context but is advantageous to the firm only if competing firms cannot mimic it and customers value what it allows the firm to offer them. Advantage is always measured relative to competitors as assessed by potential customers. In another industry, the capability on which the firm's competitive advantage is based might not provide any advantage. Similarly, although superior position is necessarily relative to competitors and sometimes attained by historical accident, it is often the outgrowth of some internal asset. Perceiving the need for money transfer services and organizing a system to deliver them, for example, suggests some capability. Furthermore, the firm's internal assets must be used to defend the position. A dominant firm, for example, will not remain dominant unless it can undercut potential competitors by upgrading service offerings or pricing aggressively. Positions Inc. and Global Capabilities each had only *one* kind of competitive advantage. We made this sharp distinction between positions and capabilities to highlight the differences between these two types of advantage. Most firms, however, have some advantages of both types, and each type reinforces the other. For now, to explain what we mean by each, we will discuss them separately. Later in this chapter we return to how they tend to be interrelated.

Position

A firm can have many specific kinds of positional advantage, but any positional advantage takes one of three main forms:

- *Positional advantage from an attractive industry structure.* Sometimes all the firms in an industry benefit from the industry's structure. For example, a duopoly, an industry with just two firms, is typically more profitable than an industry with many competing firms. In a duopoly, each firm has somehow managed to achieve a position as one of two incumbents and is likely to be profitable because it has that position. Airbus and Boeing, for example, are the only two manufacturers of large, commercial aircraft in the world, and each benefits from that position.

- *Positional advantage from heterogeneity within the industry.* Often positions within an industry create advantage for the firms occupying them. For example, a firm that has a dominant position in an otherwise fragmented industry usually does better than other industry incumbents. Large fast-food chains have been able to leverage scale economies in production and advertising that give them a competitive advantage over the competing, independent fast-food outlets. The smaller firms have higher costs and less brand equity than their dominant rivals.
- *Positional advantage from a network of relationships.* A firm may derive positional advantage from its relationships with buyers, suppliers, or competitors. For example, venture capital firms compete based on their ability to identify good investment opportunities, create pools of investment capital, and manage their investment portfolios. Within the venture capital community, a few firms have achieved a central position in the network that makes up the "deal flow." Because these firms are well-connected to other venture capitalists, investors, and entrepreneurs, they are well positioned to broker deals among them and to be compensated for their services.

Examples of Positional Advantage

There are many specific positional advantages, some of which can easily be assigned to one category. Others, however, are more complex and are derived from more than one category. The following list provides some sense of the rich variety of positional advantage.

- *Brand name:* A firm with a widely recognized and appreciated brand name has positional advantage over other firms in its industry whose brands are weaker. A strong brand lets the firm command premium shelf space, wider customer attention, and higher prices. Nike, for example, developed a very powerful global brand in sports shoes and has recently leveraged this positional advantage in shoes into related consumer products.
- *Customer relationships:* A firm with an established reputation for "fair dealing" has a positional advantage over competitors whose customers are concerned about opportunistic behavior. For example, Marks and Spencer in the United Kingdom and Nordstrom in the United States are companies that have developed strong customer relationships based in part on their reputations for no-questions-asked return policies and consistent product quality.
- *Government protection and support:* A firm can derive positional advantage from government intervention in many ways. For example, a firm may gain advantage from being the sole domestic producer in a country where the govern-

ment's commercial policies favor domestic firms. Dominion Engineering Works benefited for many years from its position as Canada's national champion in the manufacture of paper-making machinery. Its favored position gained it various subsidies and shelter from some forms of competition.

- *Status:* Investment banks that compete with one another to underwrite commercial debt issues can gain positional advantage from their status within the banking community. Banks recognized as "high status" get more opportunities to underwrite lucrative issues on better terms. When they are the lead bank of the underwriting syndicate, other banks are happy to be junior partners in the syndicate, and banks forming syndicates seek them out as syndicate partners. In both cases, the other banks are willing to make concessions to the high-status bank to gain the benefit of being associated with it.

- *Distribution channels:* A firm may have a dominant position with the major firms in its distribution channels. Procter and Gamble makes many leading consumer products that are sold through supermarkets. Because it owns many of the products that draw retail traffic, it is in a better position to persuade its channel partners to devote valuable shelf space to its new products than is a firm with a more limited product scope.

- *Geographic incumbency:* Sometimes the geographic location of a firm is a source of advantage. Wal-Mart, for example, was the first mass merchant to locate its outlets in small towns. It located its stores in areas with too few customers to support more than one large discount store. It also blanketed regions with its stores, leaving no geographic niche for a competitor to enter.

- *Installed base and de facto standards:* In markets where product compatibility is important, firms with a large installed base have a positional advantage. For example, a consumer choosing a word processing package will probably prefer one that makes her files compatible with her co-workers' files. If they use Microsoft Word®, she will probably use Microsoft Word®.

- *Gatekeepers in the flow of goods or information:* Sometimes a firm gains positional advantage from controlling a key connection between other firms or consumers. For example, consider the owner of the only bridges across a river. The need to transport goods across the river gives the bridge owner significant positional advantage. Similarly, search engines (such as Yahoo, Lycos, and others) control major points of access to information on the Internet, giving them a positional advantage they can exploit by charging advertisers for the right to be featured on their sites.

Some general characteristics of positional advantage are exemplified in this list. First, many positional advantages accrue to firms that "move first." Wal-Mart moved into small towns first, preempting an opportunity for other firms. The first venture capital firms in Silicon Valley to achieve great success became the central firms. The observation that moving early to exploit an opportunity can be advantageous is the source of the expression "first-mover advantage." Second, positional advantage is only defined *relative* to actual and potential competitors. If Procter and Gamble were one of a thousand detergent manufacturers with equal scope, it would have no positional advantage within its channels. Similarly, a firm's position in a network is only advantageous relative to the other actors (competitors, customers or suppliers) who are also members of the network.

Capabilities

Firms, like individuals, differ in their abilities. Consider a firm's ability to manufacture products at low cost. Some might be able to do this because they have special access to low-cost inputs, such as raw materials or labor, or because they are the favored recipients of government subsidies. These firms' low costs are due to positional advantages. Other firms, however, are low-cost producers because they have learned how to combine their inputs more efficiently than do other firms. Through on-going experimentation, learning, and experience, they develop methods that others lack. Their ability to process and combine inputs efficiently is a capability.

Firms possess many different kinds of capabilities. Some, like the Sony Corporation, are renowned for their ability to miniaturize consumer electronics. Indeed, Sony is the model for the fictional firm Global Capabilities. Another capability that has become increasingly important is an ability to minimize "time to market": designing and producing products quickly. For example, in the 1980s Toyota was able to design and produce a car in just three years, while the typical U.S. car manufacturer took five years. Not all capabilities, of course, relate to design and manufacturing. Merck, for example, is a leading pharmaceutical company with a capability for extraordinarily productive research and development, and LL Bean is a mail-order retailer known for its ability to provide a focused range of consumer products through an efficient and effective customer interface.

Sometimes a firm's capability is exercised repetitively for a specific process, whereas in other cases the capability has more general applications. Compare, for example, the following statements: "Sony knows how to miniaturize," and "Georgia-Pacific (GP) knows how to make high-quality check-writing paper." Georgia-Pacific's know-how refers to a specific process it has mastered to produce a particular kind of paper. Because only a handful of firms in the United States have mastered this production process, GP has a capabilities-based competitive advantage. But this ability does not, by itself, give it a competitive advantage in other products, even other kinds of paper. Indeed, this ability is so specific that GP has successfully produced check paper on only a few of its paper-making machines and has had difficulty transferring this ability to other machines even when using the same operators. In contrast, Sony's miniaturization skills enable it to miniaturize within a broad class of electronics applications (computers, stereos, televisions, etc.). This capability, for example, allowed Sony to solve the manufacturing problems associated with producing a laptop computer for Apple Computer quickly enough to satisfy intense time-to-market pressure. Sony accomplished this even though it had never before produced a laptop computer. Its success in this venture was an application of its general capability in designing and manufacturing electronic products.

Often it does not matter whether the firm's capability is specific know-how related to a given process or a more general capability. Sometimes, however, it matters a lot. To understand why, consider what will happen to Georgia Pacific and Sony if some change in their environment makes their current products obsolete. If Georgia Pacific no longer has a market for check paper, its check paper know-how will be worthless because it cannot be used for other products. In contrast, Sony's capability gives it an ability to compete in a broad range of products; it is therefore less vulnerable to environmental changes and better able to take advantage of new opportunities. If the market is no longer interested in miniaturized mobile tape players, it may still be interested in miniaturized computers.

Often, the firm's most valuable capabilities are an attribute of the firm as an organization; that is, it is not possible to separate the capability from the firm. Expertise is dispersed through many parts of the firm, and the organization has routines that access and coordinate that information. In this case, we can say that the capability is an attribute *of the organization*. As an example, consider a fire department's firefighting capability. When an emergency call comes in, the dispatcher decides which fire stations to alert based on the location and severity of the blaze. At each alerted station, the firefighters automatically fill a variety of roles, often with no need to communicate among themselves. Based on the information received, various teams assemble in their preassigned positions on specific equipment that is appropriate to the circumstance. On reaching the fire, the firefighters again perform many tasks habitually and without explicit direction from others. When unexpected or particularly complex contingencies require on-site evaluation, a chain of command and routines for making and carrying out decisions governs the team's behavior.

In this example, as in most cases of organizational capabilities, elements of individual know-how and ability play a role. More important, however, are the organizational routines, the hierarchy that determines formal authority, and the formal procedures and informal rules that the team has developed to enable it to carry out its complex tasks almost automatically. A firefighter who leaves the team is relatively easy to replace; the team only suffers a temporary loss of efficiency before the replacement can take up where his predecessor left off. The capability survives the individual members because the organizational glue that embodies the capability does not depend on any individual.

Although latent capabilities may provide a *potentially* rich source of competitive advantage, they are not in themselves a competitive advantage. The firm needs to apply the capability in a specific setting to realize the competitive advantage. It must also be able to exercise them in a market where they are superior to the capabilities of most of the actual and potential competitors it faces there. Even the most impressive capabilities are not a source of competitive advantage if most competing firms can match them. When a firm has actually demonstrated its competitive prowess by performing a set of activities better than its rivals can, the specific application of the capability is sometimes called a *distinctive competence*.

Examining a firm's distinctive competences is a good starting point for identifying what capabilities the firm possesses. This is useful, generally speaking, because it is harder to recognize competitive advantages based on capabilities than those based on position. Often positional advantages are fairly easy to identify and well known to the decision makers in the firm. The firm's capabilities tend to be harder to identify. Moreover, the strategy literature is more divided over what the important classes of capabilities are and how one should catalog and measure them. Thus it is usually easiest to identify valuable capabilities by starting with the areas in which the firm has already demonstrated success, and then to uncover the capabilities underlying them. For example, starting with Sony's distinctive competence in the design and manufacture of consumer electronics, one would go on to uncover its underlying capabilities in miniaturization and design-for-manufacture.

A serious pitfall in assessing capabilities is maintaining objectivity. In a study of the simpler task of assessing a firm's current competitive strengths and weaknesses, Stevenson[2] found that managers had widely differing views of their distinctive competencies. As Grant[3] has observed, "Organizations frequently fall victim to past glories, hopes for the future, and wishful thinking. Among the failed industrial companies of both America and Britain are many which believed themselves world leaders with superior products and customer loyalty." As he notes, systematically comparing the firm's capabilities with those of its competitors is one way to guard against this kind of misperception.

3.4 SUSTAINABLE COMPETITIVE ADVANTAGE

We will have more to say about position and capabilities and their relationship to one another shortly. First, however, we should note that *competitive advantage is not necessarily enduring*: A firm's competitive advantages may erode over time. It is in the very nature of competition that rivals attempt to duplicate or eliminate a firm's competitive advantage. For example, once outsiders recognize that its capabilities earn Global Capabilities superior returns, existing rivals or new entrants will attempt to understand and reproduce those capabilities, or find new miniaturization and design-for-manufacturing techniques that give *them* competitive advantage over Global Capabilities.

When the sources of competitive advantage resist competition, the competitive advantage is said to be *sustainable*.[4] The major threat to the sustainability of an advantage based on capabilities is the possibility that a rival can diagnose and duplicate or make obsolete your competitive advantage. A firm can lose positional advantage because some other firm moves into the same position or because the value of the position itself is destroyed.

---

[2] Howard H. Stevenson, "Defining Corporate Strengths and Weaknesses," *Sloan Management Review* (1976), 51–68.

[3] Robert M. Grant, "The Resource-Based Theory of Competitive Advantage: Implications for Strategy Formulation," *California Management Review* (Spring 1991), 114–135.

[4] For more on sustainable advantage, see Pankaj Ghemawat, "Sustainable Advantage," *Harvard Business Review* (September-October 1986), pp. 53–58.

Capability as Sustainable Competitive Advantage

If a firm's competitive advantage is based on its capabilities, a sustainable advantage requires either that imitation is difficult or that the firm can improve its capabilities (learn) before its rivals catch up. In the former case, the source of the competitive advantage must be difficult for others to understand or duplicate. In the latter case, competitors may always be imitating the leader, but the leader is always moving ahead. These kinds of learning advantages are a good example of a competitive advantage based on both capability and position. The firm's initial advantage may have arisen because it was an early entrant to the industry. To sustain this initial positional advantage, however, the firm has to learn at a competitive rate.

Some capability-based competitive advantages are difficult to imitate even when rivals know that a firm possesses them. The problem is one of *causal ambiguity:* the difficulty for those outside (or even those inside) the organization to identify exactly what leads the organization to have the capability-based advantage. The difficulty of imitating Sony's capability in miniaturization is illustrative. It is relatively easy to see that Sony has a competitive advantage in creating compact consumer goods. It is also relatively easy to surmise that this advantage is based on design and manufacturing capabilities. But what are these capabilities? More precisely, what elements or combination of elements of Sony's internal context generate these capabilities? A competitor could adopt Sony's mission and vision statements, hire away some of Sony's key engineers, adopt its organizational and human resource policies, and imitate its plant and equipment. But the competitor could probably not duplicate Sony's capability in miniaturization.

As illustrated in Figure 3-2, causal ambiguity has at least two underlying determinants. The first is the complexity of structures, routines, and individual attributes that combine to produce the capability-based advantage. It is not enough to copy some of the elements of the firm's context in isolation. And it is difficult to know which ones must be adopted together to achieve the desired ends because it is difficult to identify how the elements interact. We noted this problem in the description of Global Capabilities. Rivals had adopted its information technology system but had been unable to match its capabilities.

In addition to complexity, causal ambiguity also arises because much of the knowledge underlying a capability-based advantage is often *tacit.* Tacit knowledge is knowledge that is uncodified. Tacit knowledge is not written down. Moreover, in general, it is extremely difficult to communicate if only because those possessing it typically do not rationalize their behavior. A classic example of tacit knowledge is a ship captain's knowing where and how to fish in the deep sea. A passenger aboard the captain's ship may imitate every behavior he sees the captain undertake and still be unable to match the captain's yield. Even the captain may not be able to articulate completely all the behaviors that give him or her a superior capability in finding and catching fish, at least partly because those behaviors are internalized. They are taken-for-granted. The captain simply does not need to think about each and every behavior that enhances his or her fishing ability. Organizations renowned for superior customer service also find that their capability is grounded as much in tacit as in overt knowledge.

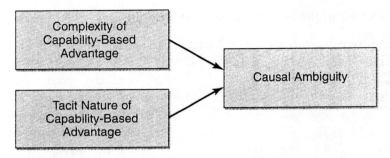

FIGURE 3-2 Sources of Causal Ambiguity

Their employees simply take a strong customer orientation for granted and do not dissect every individual behavior that sustains that advantage.

To provide sustainable competitive advantage, a capability must not be "owned" by a small group of employees, or it can literally walk away from the firm. If a firm's ability to design microprocessors depends only on the knowledge and skill of key people, that capability can leave the firm with those people. If a fishing vessel's catch depends on the ability of the ships' captain, the owner of the boat does not own the ability to catch fish.

Even if the valuable asset doesn't leave the firm, those who control it may be able to extract much of the value it creates because they can *threaten* to walk away. For example, movie stars can extract much of the value that is created when a syndicate is formed to make a film in which they star even if they do not explicitly own a share of the syndicate. A substantial share of the value of the film can be attributed to the brand name and ability of its leading actors, and they will bargain to capture as much of that value as possible. One reason for the Disney Corporation's success might be that its animated stars cannot leave: Mickey Mouse extracts none of the value he creates for Disney! The creative staff responsible for creating and extending Mickey can leave, but the capability of creating animated films depends on many people and on a set of organizational routines and structures that are embedded in the organization itself. It is an attribute of the organization, not of individual know-how.

Position as Sustainable Competitive Advantage

An advantageous position can be sustainable, but frequently it is not. Positions Inc.'s advantage seems to be sustainable because its network of offices has given it an enduring advantage relative to potential entrants. Although the industry is attractive for the established firm, it appears to be unattractive for a second firm to enter. To offer a competing network, a rival must open branches in many cities. Thus the entry costs are significant. At the same time, entry would trigger fierce competition with Positions Inc. because Positions Inc. strategically prices to discourage entry.

AT&T's data transmission network or IBM's installed base in mainframe computers might be other examples of sustainable positional advantage. An installed base can be a durable advantage because overcoming it requires that customers be at a disadvantage while the firm "catches up." Suppose I want to start a firm that will compete with IBM. Even if the first customer who buys from me gets hardware as good as IBM's central processing unit, she will have no established base of peripheral manufacturers or software application developers from whom to buy products. These third parties will not design products compatible with my mainframe until I sell enough of them to make their investment in product development worthwhile. But I can't sell enough until they make the investment. This chicken-and-egg problem presents a formidable barrier to anyone interested in challenging IBM.

In contrast, many domestic firms that depended on trade barriers found their positional advantage disappeared when trade barriers were dropped. With high trade barriers blocking direct investment by foreign firms, the domestic banks in Korea exploited their position as domestic firms to earn attractive returns. As the trade barriers were lowered, these firms found they had no capability-based advantage to protect them once their positional advantage was lost. The value of the domestic banks' position was destroyed when entry became feasible.

In other cases, the position retains its value, but *the firm occupying it changes*. In the 1990s, the only firm licensed to provide direct satellite broadcasting (DSB) to televisions in the United Kingdom was unexpectedly challenged by a new entrant using an unregulated technology. The system costs for DSB are so high that only one firm could profitably serve the market. This is a market structure known as a "natural monopoly." The two firms struggled to win the monopoly position, incurring huge operating losses. In the end, the first firm was forced to give in and was purchased by its competitor. This kind of battle can occur only because it is the *position itself* that is valuable. Similarly, in the case of IBM's dominant position in mainframe computers, IBM's status as the industry standard was valuable. Because all third-party suppliers of complementary hardware and software want to support the dominant design and all consumers want to buy it, smaller players struggled to survive. In this situation, it may not be possible to be a successful niche player; the only way to compete successfully might be to replace IBM as the standard.

3.5 THE RELATIONSHIP OF POSITION TO CAPABILITIES

Although we have found it useful to describe position and capabilities as though they are distinct sources of competitive advantage and, indeed, have illustrated them largely through examples in which they *are* distinct, position and capabilities usually interact to produce competitive advantage for the firm as illustrated in Figure 3-3.

Cisco Systems, for example, is the dominant supplier of computer networking hardware. It has capabilities in the underlying technologies that helped it attain its dominant position, but it has also leveraged its position to obtain complementary technologies developed at other firms through an aggressive acquisitions program. The fact that it was an early mover in network infrastructure also allowed it to build a position that would have been more difficult for it to attain later. Looking at the firm now, we find it very difficult to decide exactly how much of its advantage is positional and how much is based on its capabilities.

Nonetheless, it is frequently useful for managers to understand whether their firm's competitive advantage is based primarily on position or on capabilities. A pri-

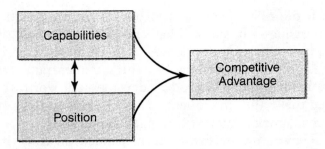

FIGURE 3-3 Capabilities and Position Interact

mary reason to identify the firm's sources of competitive advantage is to alert its management to those attributes that must be protected and exploited if the firm is to succeed. Consider, for example, the owner of a coffee shop that is successful only because it happens to have a prime location. If its manager mistakenly believes she has some particular facility at management or a strong brand name and opens new stores based on that belief, she is likely to be disappointed. If the managers of Global Capabilities had not recognized that its design and manufacturing success with its first products was the result of a capability that could be widely applied, it might never have expanded beyond its initial base as a maker of electronic calculators. If the managers of Positions Inc. decide to compete in electronic fund transfer over the Internet using their brand name and technological expertise, they will make a serious mistake.

Some analysts go further, arguing that whether a firm conceives of its competitive advantage in terms of position or capabilities fundamentally affects how it perceives the opportunities it faces. This line of argument is perhaps made most forcefully in an article by Prahalad and Hamel[5] in which they suggest that managers should think of their firm as defined by its capabilities rather than by its products. Xerox, for example, has recently tried to recast its public image from a manufacturer of copiers to a firm that manages documents. A firm that views itself in terms of positional advantage will tend to view its opportunities relative to its existing product line. For example, it may think about ways to reposition its current products, to enhance them, or to extend the existing family of products incrementally. A firm that conceives of itself in terms of capabilities, however, may be inclined to think more broadly about ways to leverage its existing capabilities into products it has not previously considered. For example, a natural way for the Boeing Corporation to conceive of itself is in terms of its product line, predominantly aircraft. An alternative conception might focus on Boeing's extraordinary capabilities in managing complex, large-scale projects (of which aircraft manufacture is one). Such a conception might usefully open the door to opportunities Boeing might not otherwise have considered.

Although the idea that a firm should be defined as a bundle of capabilities is useful for managers developing the firm's strategies, it is also easy to abuse. It is tempting to define these capabilities too broadly. For example, it is currently popular to describe

---

[5] C. K. Prahalad and Gary Hamel, "The Core Competence of the Corporation," *Harvard Business Review* (May–June 1990), pp. 79–91.

firms as providers of "business solutions." The intent seems to be to emphasize that the firm has the capability to solve a broad spectrum of business problems. But the term is used so widely that it hardly has any content. Truck manufacturers, financial institutions, maintenance companies, and information technology outsourcing firms have all described themselves as providers of business solutions. In addition, a view of the firm's capabilities as its sole or major source of competitive advantage neglects the fact that any existing positional advantage that the firm has achieved through those capabilities may be more valuable than the potential advantage the capabilities might yield elsewhere. Positions Inc. may have had an unusual capability for organizing a geographically dispersed firm when it was first established. But by now, that capability is common, and only the firm's position is valuable.

3.6 POSITION, CAPABILITIES, AND "THE RESOURCE-BASED VIEW OF THE FIRM"

Despite the importance of understanding competitive advantage, most early treatments of the determinants of firm performance simply distinguished between "internal" and "environmental" factors. Moreover, the treatment was typically superficial, consisting of a listing of strengths and weaknesses. This changed with the publication of Michael Porter's *Competitive Strategy* in 1980. Drawing on a rich body of theoretical and empirical research in the subfield of economics known as Industrial Organization, Porter demonstrated the importance of thoroughly understanding the firm's *industry and its competitive position within it*. That book in turn helped fuel a flurry of research activity and writing on analyzing the firm's external context. At the same time, economists were using the tools of applied game theory to develop a more systematic understanding of a firm's interactions with its rivals and with other participants in the value chain. As a consequence, the 1980s was a period in which researchers focused predominantly on the external environment. This research has produced an important body of knowledge to which we shall return in later chapters. But its success contributed to the neglect of the internal and organizational determinants of firm performance.

By the early 1990s, however, a series of articles in strategic management had reasserted the importance of considering factors internal to the firm when searching for the source of heterogeneous firm performance. Articles by Wernerfeld, Barney, and Montgomery,[6] for example, revived the ideas of Edith Penrose[7] stressing a "resource-based" view of the firm. As the name suggests, the resource-based view of the firm emphasizes the firm's internal resources as a source of potential competitive advantage. To the extent that a firm's capabilities are based on its resources—its routines and organization, for example—the resource-based view certainly encompasses capabilities. To the extent that a firm's positional advantage is based on its tangible and

---

[6] See, for example, Birger Wernerfeld, "A Resource Based View of the Firm," *Strategic Management Journal* 5 (1984) 171–180; Jay B. Barney, "Strategic Factor Markets: Expectations, Luck, and Business Strategy," *Management Science* 42 (1986) 1231–1241; and Cynthia Montgomery and Birger Wernerfeld, "Diversification, Ricardian Rents, and Tobin's q," *Rand Journal of Economics* 19 (1988) 623–632.

[7] Edith T. Penrose, *The Theory of the Growth of the Firm* (New York: Wiley, 1958).

intangible assets, the resource-based view can also be interpreted as pushing for a deeper understanding of the underlying internal sources of the firm's positional advantage. And this has created a more balanced view of competitive advantage as arising from a combination of internal and external factors.

However, using the resource-based view to justify a focus *on the firm's assets in and of themselves* is a mistake. The resources are a source of competitive advantage only if they create positional advantage or advantageous capabilities. To see what we mean consider a third hypothetical company which, like Positions Inc. and Global Capabilities, also has superior performance:

Resources Associates is a medical device manufacturer. The founder and current CEO, a former university professor, patented a process for producing a specialized medical instrument. Convinced that the founder's knowledge of the process provides it with a competitive advantage in manufacturing, Resources Associates makes all its own devices, selling them through sales agents to medical equipment distributors. Industry sources say that Resources Associates' cost of goods sold is slightly lower than its competitors'. Resources Associates has refused several offers to buy the company (offers the founder viewed as attempts to rob him of the value of his invention). The firm has also consistently refused to license its patented technology, fearing it would sacrifice the firm's competitive advantage if it did.

In contrast to Global Capabilities, Resources Associates does not seem to be particularly good at manufacturing (since it has only a slight cost advantage in production despite proprietary ownership of a superior, patented manufacturing process). In fact, it does not seem to have any identifiable capabilities. For example, it has none in the sales and distribution areas (it outsources these functions). Rather, the key determinant of Resources Associates' success is its patent for producing a particular piece of medical equipment. Without that patent, Resources Associates' financial performance would likely be mediocre, or worse. In this case, the firm's competitive advantage derives from its possession of an asset that no other firm can acquire without its consent. Its proprietary technology enables the firm to be low-cost, thereby creating a positional advantage over its rivals. The patent ensures that a competitor cannot simply acquire the technology.

Although scarce and proprietary assets like Resource Associates' patent are valuable, owning them is not a sufficient basis for building a high-performance organization. Resources Associates' value is derived solely from its asset, and that asset is separable from the firm and tradable. Because Resources Associates has no complementary manufacturing and distribution abilities, the founder could probably do better by selling the patent to a firm that does have these capabilities. The firm that purchased the patent would then have the positional advantage, and Resources Associates would have none. If strategy is about guiding action to maximize performance given the firm's context, the only strategic choice that makes sense for Resources Associates is to sell its asset to the highest bidder. In other cases, the firm owning the asset may have *other* capabilities or a positional advantage that makes it the organization best able to take advantage of this asset. Even in this case, however, these additional assets by themselves might not provide the firm with a competitive advantage *absent* ownership of the scarce resource. Even if Positions

Inc. also owned an efficient manufacturing operation, for example, it might be unable to distinguish itself among other device manufacturers without the patented process.

Economists call the value that the owner can capture from a scarce asset the *rent* from the asset. It is useful, where possible, to identify which component of a firm's superior performance is simply a rent to a scarce asset that it owns. For Resources Associates, the value that the firm is able to create and capture is simply the rent from its patent. Similarly, to return to the example of the coffee shop, a proprietor of a coffee shop who owns the land on which it is located may have a spectacular rate of return compared to the many other shops with which he competes. Yet, that return is appropriately attributed to the value of the land not to the shop, and the superior financial performance of the coffee shop would likely disappear if, as landowner, she charged herself an appropriate rent for the land.

These examples are introduced to make two distinct points about resources as a source of competitive advantage. First, it is important to recognize when a firm's superior performance is simply due to a rent earned on some asset. It is dangerous, for example, for a firm to attribute its superior performance to its superior manufacturing or marketing capabilities if indeed those capabilities are ordinary and its superior performance is the rent earned from its location, patent, or brand name. Second, it is a mistake to think of a firm as simply a bundle of resources or assets, ignoring the external context. It is this narrow focus that encouraged the founder of Resource Associates to create a firm with a meager competitive advantage rather than selling the asset to another owner to whom it would be more valuable. An organization creates value when it can deploy its assets so that they are more valuable under its control than they would be elsewhere. Often, as many of our previous examples have suggested, this is because the firm has some capability that enables it to use those assets in ways others cannot replicate.

3.7 THE COST–QUALITY FRONTIER AND COMPETITIVE ADVANTAGE

We have emphasized that competitive advantage flows from superior capabilities or position or from some combination of the two. We have taken this approach because we believe that it is vital for an organization to understand the source of its competitive advantage if it is to build on and defend it. To make our point, we have talked about many specific forms of positional and capability-based advantages. Having done so, we can now explore two general dimensions in which competitive advantage often can be summarized: cost and quality. A firm may have lower costs than other firms producing similar products or more valuable products than firms with similar costs. In either case, its superior performance flows from being well positioned in cost and quality dimensions.

Inasmuch as superior performance is based on a firm's ability to create and capture value, it is not surprising that a firm's competitive advantage frequently can be represented by its cost–quality position. A firm creates value only when there is a difference (preferably large) between what customers are willing to pay for its products or services and what the firm must pay to provide them.[8] What customers are willing to pay is related to the quality of the firm's products. What the firm must pay to provide the product is the firm's cost. Since creating value is about generating a gap between customer valuation and the cost of providing the product, quality and cost are often useful ways to describe competitive advantage.

Because cost and quality are so commonly the dimensions in which competitive advantage can be described, it is useful to have a framework for examining competitive advantage in those terms. The framework developed in this section will be used in subsequent chapters to discuss how changes in rivals' positions can pose a competitive threat, to determine how a firm can make strategic investments in capabilities and position in order to change its competitive advantage, and to examine the relationship between organizational structure and competitive advantage. We begin by defining what we mean by "high quality" and "low cost" and then present a framework that captures the basic tradeoff between these advantages.

Remember, however, that the advantage represented by these dimensions is itself derived from some combination of capability and position. For quality, for example, it may be the firm's reputation for reliability, durability, or after-sales service (positional advantages) that makes its offerings more attractive than those of other firms in the industry. Or the firm may have superior capabilities in quickly bringing new products to market, so that its products are more advanced than its rivals'. On the cost side, the firm may have superior access to raw materials or the ability to share costs with another part of the company (positional advantages), or, like Global Capabilities, it may have developed a set of routines that lowers its overall development costs. In short, although cost and quality are a useful shorthand for thinking about a firm's competitive position, they usually derive from some asset that the firm must nurture and protect.

Product Quality and Cost

Think of two products within a well-defined product category. If all customers buy one of them when the two are offered at identical prices, the chosen product has a higher perceived quality.[9] To use a more concrete example, consider pens. BIC and Mont Blanc are both well-known brand names in the pen market with clear and distinct images. BIC pens are reliable, inexpensive, functional writing instruments. Mont Blanc pens are made with more costly materials, are designed to be durable, are engineered to write more smoothly, and are associated with higher socioeconomic status. Mont Blanc's advertising uses words like "elegant" and "distinctive." Most consumers would agree that Mont Blanc pens are higher quality than BIC pens. More people buy

---

[8] If one thinks of this in income statement terms, operating margin can be increased only by increasing revenue for given costs, or decreasing costs for given revenue. In economic terms, profit can only be increased by increasing the distance between the demand and cost curves for the firm's products.

[9] As we will see in Chapter 6, products about which consumers agree on quality rankings are referred to as "vertically" differentiated. We discuss product differentiation in Chapter 7.

BIC because they are unwilling to pay the price premium Mont Blanc charges for its pens, but even these people would usually agree that BIC is lower quality. Put slightly differently, if most of us were offered the choice of a Mont Blanc pen or a BIC pen as a gift, we would choose the Mont Blanc.

Many other products or services also have this characteristic. Manufacturers who buy ball bearings rank quality in terms of delivery times and defect rates. Travelers prefer airlines with better on-time departure records. Computer users prefer faster hard drive access to slower hard drive access. Sprint, a long-distance carrier, advertises itself as having better sound quality ("You can hear a pin drop"). Thinking carefully about these examples suggests that the quality ranking may be a composite of many characteristics: Travelers care about on-time departures, safety, comfort, and other dimensions of product quality, for example. It is nonetheless helpful to think about combining these dimensions into a single measure of perceived quality.[10]

Note the importance of the modifier "perceived" here. It is often tempting to think of quality as determined by the physical characteristics of the product as an engineer might define them. Thinking of quality in this way, however, misses the point. Higher quality can confer a competitive advantage on a product only if potential buyers *perceive* it to have higher quality. If a clever brand manager can convince consumers that water from springs in the Alps is better than water from springs in the Rockies, he will create a quality advantage for his product. If consumers cannot perceive a quality difference between audio systems despite the fact that electronic testing reveals that one is clearly superior at sound reproduction, the two systems have the same quality.

Just as product quality can differ in many ways, any student of cost accounting knows that the way costs are measured is open to interpretation and depends ultimately on the purpose for which the measurement is done. For our purposes, we have in mind a measure of average cost, which includes the typical expenses that go into cost of goods sold (production labor costs, materials, etc.), *and* design and marketing costs, appropriately amortized over the products sold. The reason for this, as will become clear shortly, is that in order to differentiate one's product or service offerings it may be necessary to make substantial, fixed investments in advertising, product development, and so forth. Because these costs are essential to attaining the firm's quality position, we want them reflected in our measure of cost.

Before we became enmeshed in the details of how we were defining "low cost" and "perceived quality," we claimed that these two factors could summarize competitive advantage. It is obvious why having low cost can be advantageous. A firm with lower costs for the same product will be able to price lower than its rivals, thereby capturing a larger market share while earning a margin at least as attractive as theirs. Alternatively, a low-cost firm can charge the same price as its rivals and earn a substantially higher margin on what it sells. Although the benefit of lower cost typically is realized through its impact on price, it is important to understand that it is the low

---

[10] Careful thought also suggests that not all products are well characterized in this way. Sometimes consumers don't agree about quality rankings. Some people prefer Coke to Pepsi, others Pepsi to Coke. We will return to this type of differentiation in Chapter 7 and discuss how the framework we develop here would apply to that case.

cost that is the competitive advantage and not the low price per se. Quality can be a competitive advantage because a product perceived to be higher quality can command a price premium. If the products have the same cost, the higher quality product has a clear competitive advantage. The higher quality firm has the choice of charging the same price as its rival and capturing a very large market share or charging more and making a higher margin on its sales.

If both lower cost and higher quality can be competitive advantages, it is tempting to conclude that the best overall position is to be a high-quality, low-cost firm. In principle, this is correct. In fact, it is usually not possible. The Rolls Royce managers would be overjoyed to produce its cars for a cost lower than that achieved by Chevrolet. And any four-star restaurant owner would be delighted to produce its meals at the same cost as McDonald's. The problem, of course, is that high quality and low cost are frequently in conflict. A handcrafted walnut and leather automobile interior is more costly to produce than a vinyl and molded plastic interior. Paté and arugula cost more than chopped beef and french fries. Firms that are operating efficiently face an inevitable tradeoff between cost and quality.

A Cost–Quality Framework

Figure 3-4 illustrates what we mean when we say there is an inevitable tradeoff between cost and quality. In this diagram, quality is measured on the vertical axis and cost on the horizontal. Note that cost *decreases* along the horizontal axis; that is, the farther we move to the right, the lower the cost. Cost is represented in this way so that the firm is better off in both quality and cost the farther it is positioned from the origin.

The shaded region of this diagram indicates all the quality and cost combinations that are feasible given currently available technology. By technologically available, we mean not just to the firm but to the industry more generally. It is easy to produce at any point near the origin, well in the interior of the shaded region. Any such point represents a combination of low quality and high costs—not a difficult position to

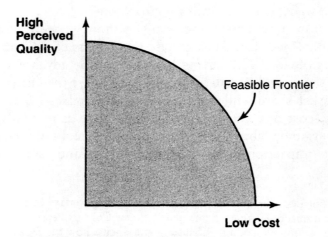

FIGURE 3-4 The Cost and Perceived Quality Framework

attain. As one moves away from the origin, however, the cost–quality combinations become increasingly challenging to attain because they involve lower costs and/or higher levels of quality.

The curved edge of the shaded region represents the limits of what is available with current technology. This line identifies the highest quality that can be provided for a given cost. Conversely, it identifies the lowest cost at which a product of a given quality can be provided. We therefore call this line the "cost–quality frontier." Points beyond the frontier are simply not achievable given the current technology at the disposal of the firms in the industry. Any firm would like to be able to go boldly where no firm has gone before, but this is simply not possible with the best available technology.

The frontier is a downward-sloping curve because along it there is a tradeoff between perceived quality and low cost: Higher-quality products (produced as efficiently as possible) cost more to produce than lower-quality ones (produced as efficiently as possible). Starting at any given point on the frontier, perceived quality can only be increased by expending additional effort and resources, that is, by increasing costs. For some readers, this assertion flies in the face of examples in which firms have been able to increase perceived quality while holding cost constant or even reducing them. This is possible in two circumstances. Most commonly, it means the firm was not initially operating on the frontier. As noted above, a firm located near the origin has lots of room to improve quality without increasing its cost.[11] Less commonly, the firm achieves some technological breakthrough that changes the frontier. We will return to this possibility later in the book. Here we assume that the frontier is fixed.

The concave shape of the frontier we've drawn reflects an assumption that additional cost has a diminishing effect. That is, at the point the frontier intersects with the cost axis, it is relatively inexpensive to increase perceived quality, but as you move in a northwesterly direction, any given quality improvement becomes increasingly costly. Imagine, for example, what it costs to substantially improve the quality of a premier bordeaux wine compared to improving the quality of a mass-produced jug wine! While we think that this is a reasonable assumption for many products, it is not essential to the framework. What is essential is that the frontier be downward sloping.

Using the Cost–Quality Frontier to Illustrate Competitive Advantage: An Example

Suppose we are analyzing the hotel industry in the United States and have data that suggest that the hotels are situated at points A, B, and C in Figure 3-5. Point A might represent a hotel like the Ritz Carlton that prides itself on its luxurious accommodation and service. Point C might represent a budget chain of hotels, such as the Travelodge or Quality Inn, that prides itself on providing affordable, if basic, accommodations with little service. Point B might represent an intermediate chain, such as the Sheraton. As suggested by their relationship to the vertical axis, most con-

---

[11] We do not mean to minimize the managerial and organizational commitment necessary to be on the frontier. Indeed, few firms are so efficient that they are clearly on the frontier. It is nonetheless important to recognize that improving quality and reducing cost are usually conflicting objectives for *reasonably* efficient firms.

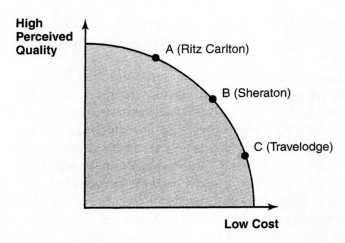

FIGURE 3-5 Using the Cost-Quality Framework to Map Competition

sumers would rank the perceived quality of the hotels as the Ritz, followed by the Sheraton, followed by the Travelodge.

There is nothing disparaging about positioning the Travelodge in this way. Indeed, putting any hotel on the frontier is a compliment because it says that it is being as efficient as possible in providing its level of perceived quality.

Conversely, there is nothing disparaging about observing that the Ritz has higher costs than the Travelodge. It is simply a fact of life in the hotel industry that creating and sustaining a perceived quality of the kind associated with the Ritz is more costly. The furnishings and decor, hotel locations, hours of room service availability, promotional materials, and so on, are all more expensive for an exclusive hotel than for a budget hotel. If it were possible to create a Ritz Carlton experience for the cost of a Travelodge experience, this quality diversity would not exist in the marketplace: Every hotel would be like the Ritz and price like the Travelodge. Quality diversity exists precisely because there is a tradeoff between perceived quality and cost, as assumed in the figure.

Since the Ritz Carlton and the Travelodge are at the extremes of the frontier (at least in our example), it is tempting to articulate their strategies in terms of just the dimension at which they excel—that is, to represent the Ritz's strategy as being one of high perceived quality and the Travelodge's as one of low cost. Indeed, some strategic management texts follow Michael Porter's lead and argue that high quality and low cost are distinct and generic strategies.[12] This treatment, however, glosses over an important point about the competitive advantage of firms on the frontier. Yes, the Ritz is higher quality than Travelodge and, by necessity, has higher cost than the Travelodge. But the Ritz in our example is as low cost as possible *given* that it produces a high-quality product. The Travelodge produces a product that is as high quality as possible *given* that it has low cost.

---

[12] Michael E. Porter, *Competitive Strategy* (New York: Free Press, 1980).

An even more important problem with claiming that "high quality" and "low cost" are the clear positions of competitive advantage is that these polar cases need not provide performance superior to an intermediate position. Consider the Sheraton's position. The strategy represented by the Sheraton in the figure is an intermediate one. It is neither as high quality as the Ritz Carlton nor as low cost as the Travelodge. At the same time, its costs are not as high as the Ritz Carlton nor its quality as low as the Travelodge. This enables the Sheraton to position itself on the frontier "between" its more extreme rivals. The fact that its costs are lower than the Ritz enables it to price lower, attracting customers who want higher perceived quality than the Travelodge offers at a price lower than that of the Ritz. If this position appeals to enough hotel visitors, it could be the most profitable position on the frontier. More generally, there is a continuum of cost and quality positions on the frontier, and there is no reason to believe that occupying either the high-quality or the low-cost position is the only possible way to achieve competitive advantage.

On the other hand, contrast the Sheraton's position with that of Hotel D (which we will not name because to do so *would be* disparaging!) in Figure 3-6. Hotel D is in an unfavorable position. Although its perceived quality is higher than that of the Travelodge and its costs are lower than the Ritz Carlton, it is in an inferior position on both dimensions to a hotel like the Sheraton. In a reasonably competitive industry, such a firm would not be expected to last very long. Given its superior positioning, the Sheraton would be expected to offer a superior experience at a lower price than Hotel D could. As consumers learn of this fact, Hotel D will steadily lose market share to the Sheraton and finally be driven out of business. The Sheraton's position on the frontier gives it competitive advantage in both cost and quality over Hotel D. A hotel located at any point in the cross-hatched region in Figure 3-6 is at a competitive disadvantage to the Sheraton.

Although firms on the frontier have a competitive advantage over firms in the interior, these latter firms may be viable. If, for example, D is in an industry with high barriers to entry and faces only a few competitors, such as A and C, it may be able to

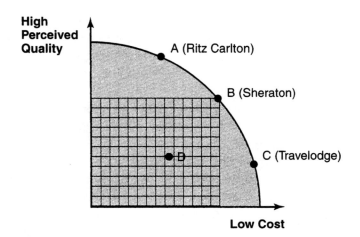

FIGURE 3-6 Firm B Has a Competitive Advantage over Firm D

survive thanks to the lack of competition from a firm like B. Nonetheless, such a position is precarious. If a firm manages to surmount the entry barriers and adopts a position like B, or if firm A or C decides to move toward B and can do so while remaining on the frontier, firm D will be in an untenable competitive position.

The strategy literature sometimes characterizes a firm in Hotel D's position as being "stuck in the middle." This phrase is used to describe a firm that is disadvantaged relative to its rivals in terms of cost–quality positioning and certainly applies to Hotel D. Unfortunately, the term "stuck in the middle" is also sometimes applied to any firm that does not occupy an extreme position on the frontier, that is, is not at position A or C. This usage is inappropriate. As argued above, an intermediate position on the frontier is not necessarily disadvantageous. There is nothing "stuck" about the Sheraton's position. A more appropriate, but less mellifluous, phrase to describe firms that are mired in a disadvantageous cost–quality position might be "stuck inside the frontier."

Constructing a map like the one shown in Figure 3-4 is useful for several reasons. Suppose, for example, your firm is firm D. This map tells you that you have a competitive disadvantage relative to your competitors. It also tells you that you are most directly threatened by hotels represented by points B and C. Product C has much lower cost and a quality that is only slightly lower than yours. Because your products are nearly identical to theirs, competition with the hotels at C will be based primarily on price, the very dimension in which you are least well positioned to compete with them. With respect to hotels located at B, you are disadvantaged in both dimensions. Hotels at B can charge a price higher than your cost (and even higher than theirs) and force you to charge a price less than your cost to capture any market share. With respect to those hotels, firm D is in the unenviable position of a local bar that resorted to advertising "Warm beer, bad service, moderate prices" to compete with its more fortunate rivals.

Maps like these can also provide some guidance about where the attractive openings in an industry might be. As will be argued in more detail in Chapter 7, firms that can differentiate their products from those of their competitors may benefit from reduced price competition. Suppose, for example, that no firms were located on the frontier between A and C. Then, the position denoted by B might be attractive for a new entrant or for a firm located at A or C who wanted to move away from its competitors at those locations. The firm that first recognizes this underserved part of the market may gain an important first-mover advantage by being the first to develop a product well suited to this segment.

Note, however, that such a map provides only an incomplete description of competitive advantage because it does not contain information on the distribution of demand. For example, incumbent firms may have avoided some segment of the cost–quality frontier because there is little demand for a product of that quality at a price that would cover the cost of providing it. Being on the frontier ensures that no other firm will be able to provide a higher-quality product at lower cost, but it does not ensure that buyers want to pay the cost necessary to produce a product of that quality. We will return to the topic of thinking about product positioning and the distribution of demand in Chapter 7.

3.8 SUMMARY

In this chapter we explored how the firm's capabilities and position can enable it to create and capture value, and we discussed the conditions under which the competitive advantage will be sustainable in the long run. We examined how its capabilities and position can give it competitive advantage in the form of lower costs than its rivals or the ability to differentiate its product and service offerings from theirs. Finally, we developed a cost–quality framework to illustrate a firm's competitive advantage with respect to its competitors, which will be used in later chapters.

We turn now to a discussion of how the firm is organized. We do this at this juncture because a firm's competitive advantage—especially when it derives from its capabilities—often resides in the way it is organized. In Chapter 4 we explore the components of organization and the factors that shape them. In Chapter 5 we examine the relationship of organization design to strategy and strategic change.

CHAPTER

4

INTERNAL CONTEXT: ORGANIZATION DESIGN

4.1 INTRODUCTION

A firm's competitive advantage is rooted in its context. Whether its strategic advantage is based on position or capabilities, the advantage derives from both its environment and its internal context. An advantage based on design capability, for example, is sustained by the assets and organization of the company (internal context) and by the perception of the firm's customers that its product provides better value than the products of its competitors (external context). Managers who want to create and sustain competitive advantage need, therefore, to have a deep understanding of both the internal and external context of the firm. This chapter and the next explore the firm's internal context before turning to its external context in Chapter 6. We begin with an overview of the relationship between organization design and competitive advantage before turning to a detailed examination of that relationship at Southwest Airlines. We then examine the main classes of problems organization design must address and the levers the firm has for doing so. Finally, we provide a framework, ARC analysis, for designing a high performance organization.

4.2 ORGANIZATION DESIGN AND COMPETITIVE ADVANTAGE

As illustrated in Figure 4-1, the firm's internal context is defined as its assets and the way those assets are organized. Chapter 3 provided many examples of how a firm's assets might be a source of competitive advantage. Here the focus is on achieving competitive advantage through the organization of those assets because organization is central to whether the assets are able to create competitive advantage. The importance of the organization design problem is frequently underestimated. Managers sometimes believe that having the best engineers or the best salespeople is enough to make a firm effective. Although the quality of the assets—human or physical—clearly is important to achieving competitive advantage, how those assets are organized can

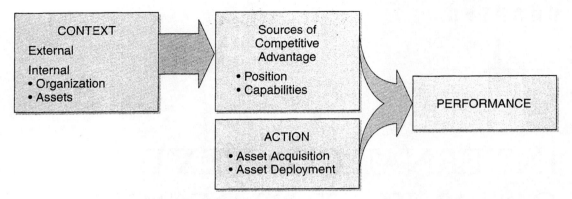

FIGURE 4-1 Sources of Competitive Advantage

be equally important. The best engineer, for example, cannot be productive if she doesn't have access to the information she needs to design products consumers value.

We have already taken issue with the claim that there is a single source of competitive advantage. We are equally skeptical about some of the popular claims that any single organization design is "best." The best design for a firm actually depends on the strategy it is pursuing. As a simple example, consider the relationship between the organization of a photo processing firm and its strategy. Most photo processing firms compete on the basis of low-cost, mass production. Boutique firms offering high-quality custom processing at correspondingly high prices occupy a different segment of the market. A typical mass-production firm is organized differently than a typical high-quality firm. Among the mass producers, the sales divisions are usually separate from the production divisions. Salespeople basically function as order-takers for a standardized product that the production unit attempts to produce as efficiently as possible. At the boutique firms, the salespeople must work much more closely with those in production to translate customer needs and to communicate the feedback from production to the customer. These firms therefore hire salespeople who know more about photography than the salespeople at the mass-production firms. But high-quality firms also establish consultation routines within the firm that facilitate communication between production and sales and supply resources for building customer relationships. The mass producers have no need for these routines or for spending resources to get to know specific customers. Furthermore, incentives at the mass producers are geared to keeping volumes high (at acceptable quality levels), while at the boutique firms, rewards are tightly tied to customer satisfaction.

This chapter provides a way to think systematically about the problem of organization design and the levers managers have to address it. Our approach is illustrated in Figure 4-2 where the internal context box is expanded to summarize the organization design challenge and the tools managers have to grapple with it. The first step in achieving competitive advantage through organization is to understand the problem that organization is supposed to solve. This overarching problem has two parts: the *coordination* problem and the *incentive* problem. Once a clear picture emerges of what the organization design should achieve, we can turn to the tools the manager has for meeting the challenge. As illustrated in Figure 4-2, a manager can work with three

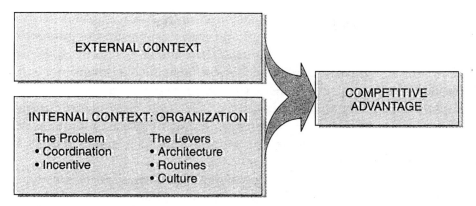

FIGURE 4-2 Organization and Competitive Advantage

levers: architecture, routines, and culture (or ARC). Before these levers and how they can be applied to address incentive and coordination problems are described, we first provide a detailed example.

4.3 STRATEGY AND ORGANIZATION AT SOUTHWEST AIRLINES

In exploring organization design, taking issues one at a time may help us understand each issue, but it sacrifices the richness of the problem managers actually face. Before proceeding with the analysis then, let's start with how one firm, Southwest Airlines, built an organization that has contributed to its competitive advantage. This example illustrates how the elements of organization design can interact and how organization and strategy can be linked.

Southwest's Strategy and Performance

By almost any measure, Southwest has been one of the most successful airlines in the United States. It is the only one to have earned a profit every year since 1973, its net margins have been the highest in the airline industry in many years, and for 20 years it had the highest stock return of *any* publicly traded firm in the United States. Southwest also stands out from its competitors in the strategy it has pursued and the organization it has created to support that strategy.

Southwest Airlines offers its customers low-cost, convenient service on selected routes. It primarily serves short-haul routes on which many of the travelers are frequent users and business travelers. The Houston-San Antonio and San Jose-Orange County (Los Angeles) markets are typical of the routes it serves. Unlike most major airlines that build their offerings around a hub-and-spoke design, Southwest offers nonstop, origin-destination flights. A hub-and-spoke system is designed to have planes from many origination points converge on the same "hub" airport at roughly the same time so that passengers can be reassigned to flights that fan out to multiple destinations. A great virtue of this system is that it tends to increase passenger loads on each flight and is therefore much more cost efficient than one in which passengers are routed nonstop from each origination point to each destination.

Bucking the trend, Southwest has achieved even lower costs on its routes. One source of its cost advantage is its high aircraft utilization rate: the number of hours a day each plane is in the air. Since its flights are not linked to a network of other flights by a common hub, any particular plane has less unavoidable downtime while it waits for the arrival of other planes. This leaves Southwest free to work on reducing the time the plane sits at the gate between flights. The airline is respected throughout the industry for consistently achieving a turnaround time of about 15 minutes. As a result, Southwest has been able to increase aircraft utilization to 11 hours per day compared to an industry average of 8 hours per day.

Part of the secret to Southwest's quick plane turnaround is its constant drive for simplicity and its success in "training" its customers to adapt to its systems. For example, unlike its competitors, Southwest has abandoned the use of tickets, does not reserve specific seats, serves peanuts instead of meals, and uses only one kind of airplane. In addition to enabling rapid turnaround, these deviations from traditional industry procedures also directly contribute to lower costs. Peanuts are cheaper than (even bad) meals. Using a single aircraft model reduces maintenance and training costs. Despite its "no frills" policy, Southwest has managed to achieve very high levels of customer satisfaction. It is the only U.S. carrier to have achieved the record of "best" in three key areas in a given month: best baggage handling, fewest customer complaints, and best on-time performance. By 1998, it had won this coveted "triple crown" 24 times.

Southwest's costs also are lower than the industry average because it has lower than average employee costs. For example, pilots often earn half as much at Southwest as at other airlines, even though they fly up to 40 percent more hours per month. Despite lower salaries, Southwest is famous for its high employee morale and the lowest employee turnover in the industry. Its route structure, simplified service, and low labor costs have given Southwest a clear cost advantage over its competitors: in the early 1990s it boasted costs of 7.1 cents per mile, compared to 10 cents or more for its larger rivals. Lower costs have translated into lower prices. As a result, Southwest typically dominates the markets it serves; it has a market share of 60 percent or more in the vast majority of the nonstop markets it serves.

Southwest's Organization

Much has been written about Southwest and the secrets to its success.[1] Although its success is in part attributed to its atypical market positioning and a classic low-cost strategy, analysts have also focused on Southwest's unique organization and the tight fit between how it is organized and how it achieves competitive advantage. For example, at the heart of Southwest's ability to turn its planes around quickly *and* keep its

---

[1] For more detailed examinations see Kevin and Jackie Frieber, *Nuts* (Bard Press, 1996): Fred Wiersema, *Customer Service* (New York: Harper Business, 1998), and Charles O'Reilly and Jeffrey Pfeffer, *Southwest Airlines*, a Stanford Graduate School of Business teaching case on which we have drawn for much of the detail here.

customers happy in the process is the cross-functional team that it assigns to each route. Many airlines strictly limit the discretion of ground crews, flight attendants, and pilots, and tightly define what employees assigned to each role can and cannot do. In contrast, Southwest encourages its teams to use discretion and to get the job done. So, for example, although Southwest's standard policy is that a plane is not to return to the gate simply because a passenger has boarded the wrong plane, the pilot can override that policy if she deems it worthwhile in a particular case. Southwest allows teams to define their members' roles and to cross these role boundaries where appropriate. It is not unusual, for example, to see flight attendants and pilots stowing bags. The airline also cross-trains managers to enable them to take on multiple tasks and to develop an overall understanding of the organization. This information allows them to understand the ramifications of the decisions they make and to communicate with all the groups in the organization.

Underlying Southwest's approach to business is a corporate culture that emphasizes having fun on the job and acting a little "zany." Recruiting favors people who are extroverts and team players and who lack industry experience. Southwest reaps advantage from the fact that its human resources policy contributes to a culture in which employees are rewarded for having fun on the job. The people who find the Southwest atmosphere appealing enjoy their jobs enough that they are willing to work for less than other airlines must pay. This policy, in conjunction with how teams are assigned to routes, also means that crews often get to know their passengers well. In part, this is because of employees' outgoing natures, but it is also because teams stick to the same routes, and many passengers fly those routes frequently. The employee selection and retention policies that favor extroverted employees and the "fun" culture that the company promotes lead to close customer relationships that are much more important in a repeat-business setting than they are in a larger network characterized by more anonymity. It is not unusual for regular customers to get birthday cards from their flight crews!

Employee discretion is also more important in a setting where employees put on a "friendly face" because flight attendants who crack jokes and sing are also expected to be more responsive to customers' problems. Stories are told and retold throughout the firm about employees who have gone far out of their way to help customers, including, in one case, flying a passenger in the employee's private plane. The fact that most Southwest employees do not have much industry background facilitates their inculcation into the firm's culture. They are more likely to adopt the Southwest way of providing customer service than are veterans of other airlines who would first have to "unlearn" their standard operating procedures.

Employees are encouraged to act like owners rather than employees, both by a corporate profit-sharing plan and by a corporate culture that encourages sharing ideas throughout the company. Stories abound about how employee suggestions have been implemented. To facilitate the transmission of ideas, the organization is very "flat" (i.e., it has few levels in its hierarchy) and informal. Senior managers are renowned for the time they spend in casual conversation with employees at all levels. Trust of senior management is extraordinarily high, and matters often resolved through contract negotiations at other firms are settled with a handshake at Southwest.

Comparisons to Other Airlines

Some observers argue that Southwest's internal context is simply better than those of its rivals and that other airlines should learn from—and replicate—what Southwest has done. Other high-performance customer service organizations often do, in fact, share many of the characteristics of Southwest's organization. For example, they are often very flat, informal organizations that have a high degree of trust among employees. These characteristics empower employees to exercise discretion to keep customers satisfied and encourage employees to pass their ideas and suggestions up to senior management who can then disseminate best practice across the firm. However, even though many firms with these characteristics are successful, it is important to recognize that not all firms, and, in particular, not all airlines, would be successful if they followed Southwest's example.

Several of Southwest's competitors have attempted to imitate some of the features of its organization but with only limited success. One problem has been that competitors have attempted to copy just some of the pieces. Thus, for example, competitors have formed cross-functional teams to improve plane turnaround times, but they have not copied other features of Southwest's organizational design that make the cross-functional teams an effective contributor to competitive advantage. They have not, for example, given these teams as much discretion in how to implement standard procedures or allowed them to make many exceptions to standard operating procedures. One reason they may not have copied all the important pieces is that it is difficult to tell which pieces *are* important. Another reason, however, is that Southwest's strategy is strikingly different from that of its competitors.

Southwest's strategy is based on point-to-point routes rather than on a hub-and-spoke network of routes. Each route in Southwest's system is therefore largely independent of the other routes. In the hub-and-spoke system used by most major airlines, any breakdown in performance on one route has repercussions that are felt throughout the system. If a Southwest flight is late on the Oakland-Los Angeles route, that might affect some other flights on that route until the time can be made up. When a flight is late arriving at a hub, the airlines faces a choice of holding all the planes the customers on the late flight are scheduled to take or leaving a plane load of customers stranded at the hub for several hours. Allowing a team responsible for one spoke to make a choice to delay a flight, then, can be costly for a hub-and-spoke system. Furthermore, an airline operating a complex hub-and-spoke network is more likely to experience unexpected and complex scheduling problems (such as when a snow storm somewhere in the system causes delays across the entire system). These problems are more efficiently resolved through standardized routines than by allowing employees responsible for single routes to make idiosyncratic decisions. In short, the discretion Southwest grants its flight teams is probably inappropriate for the route structure used by many of its competitors.

Because Southwest's routes are independent, a flight team can also control most of the variables that affect its performance. The team is not at the mercy of some large group of other employees who operate an entire network. If its flights are late, the team bears the cost of delay. The members not only must bear the ire of the passengers waiting to depart on the delayed flight, but they also must face the annoyance of the passengers who board that flight for its return trip and for its subsequent flights that day. In hub-and-spoke networks, flight teams have less control over the experience of their customers who typically fly on more than one flight to complete a trip. And their angry passengers are passed onto other, large groups of employees at a hub.

There is less interdependence among different teams at Southwest, and so monitoring team performance is more straightforward. Because every team understands that it is judged by its performance, its members have a strong incentive to pitch in and help. Some of this incentive is nonpecuniary; team members come to know and depend on each other. But Southwest also ties compensation to team performance. Pilots, for example, are paid per flight rather than per hour as is the practice at most other major airlines. They are happy to help board a flight and stow bags because it helps their team make performance goals and because it increases their compensation. At airlines where the airplane turnaround is affected by many other flights, this kind of compensation scheme is less appropriate.

Summary: Consistency and Alignment

This example emphasizes that organizations are composed of many elements, and the effect of one element may depend on the characteristics of another. Organizations have both structure and process; they are made up of ways of doing things and rewards for doing them; they have formal rules and structures and informal routines and norms. Many of these elements are interactive. The firm's informal behavioral norms modify the effect of its compensation scheme. The effectiveness of its decision making is influenced by the design of its processes for acquiring and diffusing information. Changing how activities are organized alters the incentives for cooperation across groups. It is essential, then, for the various elements to be *consistent*; they must work together. The remainder of this chapter explores the elements of organization design and how they might interact to affect performance.

Equally important, the effect of a particular organization design on firm performance depends on the strategy the firm is pursuing. Not only must the elements of the organization fit with one another, they must also fit with the strategy of the firm. We turn to the question of aligning strategy and organization in the next chapter.

4.4 THE CHALLENGE OF ORGANIZATION DESIGN

Every organization must face two main classes of problems: the coordination problem, and the incentive problem. The *coordination problem* is the challenge of designing an optimal organization even when everyone in the firm fully internalizes its goals and puts self-interest aside in helping it to pursue those goals.[2] Many coordination problems are familiar to students of operations where the focus is on designing systems

---

[2] Economists call this the "team problem" under the hypothesis that all members of a team share the same objectives.

that meet specified objectives. In our context, we use the term more broadly to mean the way the firm acquires and deploys the many assets it controls. The *incentive problem* is the challenge of inducing people whose private goals might diverge from the firm's to take actions that are consistent with achieving the firm's goals. The coordination problem encompasses the issues those managers charged with designing an organization would face if there were no incentive problem. The incentive problem encompasses the additional issues that arise because actors inside the firm typically have their own agendas and will, if the incentive problem is not solved, take actions that are not in the best interest of the firm no matter how well the organization design solves the coordination problem.

The Coordination Problem

The coordination problem is fundamental to any organization. If there were no gain to coordination, there would be no reason for firms to exist. Individuals could perform all activity by buying inputs they needed from other individuals and selling their output to those who needed it. All transactions would be handled by market exchanges, with none of the hierarchical control and coordination associated with firms. That this vision of individuals interacting only through the market is so foreign to our experience is a testament to the value of coordination. Firms exist because activity coordinated by organizations can be more efficient than activity coordinated by the market.[3]

The activity of coordination is the acquisition and allocation of the firm's assets. Assets, whether they are tangible (e.g., work-in-progress inventory, machines, or buildings) or intangible (e.g., expertise or information) need to be available in the right types and amounts in the right places for the organization to operate efficiently. Think, for example, of the huge number of resources and activities that must be coordinated to produce a typical car. A car has thousands of parts that must be combined in a specific pattern. Assembly must be coordinated to bring the desired combination together efficiently. The production process must also be responsive to the requirements of the design and sales processes if the final product is to meet customers' needs. Establishing an organization design that accomplishes the flow of assets within the firm so that it can achieve its objectives as efficiently as possible is what we mean by the coordination problem.

A central coordination problem is to balance the gains from specialization and the gains from integration. Assembly-line production in which each worker repetitively performs a very narrow task illustrates the gains from specialization. When firms with assembly-line production competed with firms that produced using skilled workers performing multiple tasks, the productivity advantage of assembly-line production gave firms using this approach a large cost advantage. In effect, each worker became incredibly proficient at a narrow set of activities, and the assembly line aggregated the efforts of the specialists. Even in the assembly-line story, however, there are gains to

---

[3] The "can be" in this sentence is important. There is a large literature on when activities should be coordinated within a firm and when they should be left to the market. Within a single firm, this problem is often encountered in the form of decisions about outsourcing. We will discuss these issues in Chapter 10.

integration. The flow of work must be managed to coordinate the work of the specialists efficiently. "Integration" here is reduced to a set of routines built into the workflow. In other examples, integration is more complex and requires that workers and units within the organization consciously work together. One unit may need to modify its output to make the other unit more productive, for example. The units may need to share information and make joint decisions to achieve the competitive advantage on which the firm depends. It may, for example, be important for the design engineers to work closely with sales managers to meet the customers' needs.

How decision-making processes are designed is another central coordination problem. In some organizations, senior managers make most strategic decisions centrally, and in others middle managers are given substantial decision-making authority. At Southwest, flight teams are assigned a great deal of decision-making authority, but at American Airlines the scope for decision making at the team level is more tightly circumscribed. A closely related coordination problem is how information flows through the organization. Some organizations have relatively open access to critical business information within the firm, and others have information systems that channel specific information to specific subsets of employees. Because decision makers need access to information, the allocation of decision rights and the design of information flows must be consistent.

The Incentive Problem

Because an organization is made up of many individuals and groups, it would be surprising to find that they all have objectives identical to those of the firm's owners. The objective of the stockholders is profit-maximization, but most employees have other concerns as well and may be willing to pursue their objectives at the expense of the firm's. For example, the design team at an advertising firm might care more about winning a Clio design award than about producing an advertisement that sells more of the client's product. Similarly, an individual manager may be more interested in the impact of his actions on his career opportunities than in the profitability of his unit or firm. Or a divisional manager, with an eye on the CEO's job, may believe that enhancing her own division's performance, even at the expense of another's, is a route to success. Regardless of the source of goal differences, an appropriate organization design must take them into account and moderate their impact on firm performance.[4]

These problems arise at the level both of the individual (i.e., the person willing to sacrifice the good of the unit to enhance his own career) and the subunit (i.e., a sub-

---

[4] The incentive problem is in a class of problems economists refer to as principal-agent problems. In these, there is some principal (the firm's stockholders, for example) who works through some agent (the managers of the firm, for example). When the objectives of the principal and the agent are inconsistent, the principal has the problem of designing the contract with the agent in a way that aligns the agent's incentives with those of the principal. The literature on incentive problems is large, and exploring it fully is beyond the scope of this book. See Baron and Kreps, *Strategic Human Resources: Frameworks for General Managers* (New York: John Wiley, 1999) and Lazear, *Personnel Economics for Managers* (New York; John Wiley, 1997) for more comprehensive discussions.

unit pursuing its own goals without regard to the profits of the firm). In the latter case, the problem arises because the members of subunits have objectives in common with each other that are inconsistent with promoting the overall performance of the firm. Since our primary concern in this chapter is to think about how the firm should organize its activities, we will focus mostly on the incentives of a subunit rather than on those of an individual. The nature of the problem and the available solutions, however, is the same whether we are thinking about an individual or a team of individuals with objectives in common.

In some respects, it is puzzling that an incentive problem exists even when we recognize that employees have concerns that are more complex than simple profit-maximization. After all, any subunit operates within a hierarchical structure that ultimately reports to a board of directors charged with representing shareholders' interests. So why aren't subunits simply told what to do?

Part of the problem, of course, is that the managers to whom the subunit reports often do not know precisely what they want the group to do. Some of the information on which the unit's decisions are properly based originates in the unit itself, for example. The sales group has more immediate and comprehensive information about the intensity of competition and the state of demand than do its superiors and should use this information in setting prices. If it observes that demand is falling or competition is becoming more intense, it should reduce prices to maximize firm profits. But if the unit is evaluated based on the number of sales made, it has an incentive to drop price regardless of the state of the market. Senior managers might then observe lower prices and an increase in sales along with a report from the sales division that prices were lowered in response to actions by competitors. This is a problem of *hidden information:* superiors simply do not have all the information possessed by those who make the decisions.

Superiors often find it difficult to observe exactly what actions the unit has taken. Although it is fairly easy to observe prices and sales, many actions are much more difficult to discern. Consider, for example, the kind of effort required for innovation. Because the innovative process is fraught with uncertainty, false starts, and unexpected outcomes, an outsider cannot know precisely how hard the unit is working at the task. Does failure after a month of effort mean that the unit wasn't working hard, or is failure simply part of the innovation process? Sometimes careful monitoring can give a reasonably good idea about what actions have been taken and whether those actions were appropriate. Often, however, even sophisticated, pervasive, and costly monitoring mechanisms produce information that is incomplete and even misleading. Collecting accurate information is made more difficult if the unit has an incentive to disguise what it is doing. When superiors cannot observe exactly what a unit is doing, there is a problem of *hidden action.*

The *incentive problem,* then, is to elicit the right amount and type of effort in the presence of hidden information and hidden action. The *coordination problem* is to achieve an efficient deployment of assets. These two problems can be described by the following metaphor. Solving the coordination problem is like building an efficient transportation infrastructure within the firm. Managers, for example, want to build a system of streets that allows employees to move information and other resources around in a way that makes them as productive as possible. Some streets should be simple two-lane roads, and others should be high-speed, limited-access highways. Some parts of the infrastructure should be nodes that are connected directly to many other parts; others need only minimal connection, and so forth. If the coordination problem is building the best road system for the tasks the firm must accomplish, the incentive problem is getting employees to use the roads. Employees, unless the incentive problem is solved, will use those parts of the infrastructure that get them where they want to be rather than where the firm wants them to be. This metaphor also implies, correctly, that these problems are interrelated; it is easier to get employees to use a road that is itself easy to travel. In the next section, we discuss the tools available to managers who must build the roads and direct the traffic.

4.5 MEETING THE CHALLENGE

The firm can manipulate many components of organization design to address the coordination and incentive problems. For example, when we think of how a firm is organized, we often think first of how it is divided into subunits. This is an important component of organization, but it is only one. How those subunits relate to one another is also important, as are the firm's formal and informal mechanisms for decision making. The organization's norms and the mechanisms for sustaining or changing them are also likely to be important, as are its compensation schemes, career ladders, and so forth. To bring order to the plethora of design elements, we have organized them into three categories as illustrated in Figure 4-3: architecture, routines, and culture (ARC).

Briefly, we define these components of organization as follows:

- **Architecture.** This includes how the firm is divided into subunits, the reporting relationships among them, the formal and informal mechanisms that link them, the hierarchical structure that governs them, and the recruiting and compensation policies applied to the people filling the positions within the organizational structure.

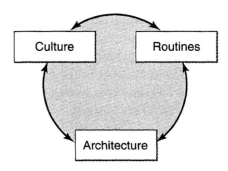

FIGURE 4-3 Elements of Organizational Design

- **Routines.** Most of the activities and decisions a firm engages in each day are similar to the ones it had to deal with the day before. The enormous amount of repetition allows a firm to develop formal and informal procedures, processes, and habits for doing the things it does. These "generally accepted methods for doing things" are the firm's routines. Many routines are neither fully codified nor even rationally determined by anyone, but evolve over time until, after much repetition, those participating in them take them for granted.
- **Culture.** "Culture" refers to the commonly held values and beliefs of individuals within the organization and, accordingly, the evaluative criteria used to make both large and small decisions.

To organize our discussion of how managers might use the levers of architecture, routines, and culture to attack the incentive and coordination problems, we first discuss each component separately. Then, in the following chapter, we turn to the problem of putting all the elements together.

Architecture: Structure

The most easily observed parts of the firm's architecture are displayed in its organization chart. The organization chart depicts the architectural *structure* that divides individuals into groups and organizes them into a governing hierarchy through reporting relationships. The architecture also includes the compensation and information systems a firm uses to evaluate individuals and groups. These latter parts of architecture are treated separately because they are used primarily to address the incentive problem. The compensation and monitoring system is one way the firm induces its employees to drive on its roads, to return to our infrastructure metaphor. The part we call structure is used primarily for addressing the coordination problem. This is about how the firm builds its road system.

Constructing an organizational structure, then, is about dividing people into subunits and defining the linkages among these groups. Some of the linkages consist of reporting relationships and channels through which superiors exercise control and allocate assets. Other linkages are horizontal, allowing subunits to function more efficiently by sharing information and resources. We begin by discussing the problem of creating subunits, and then we turn to the problem of linking them.

Because communication and resource sharing are more easily accomplished *within* subunits than *across* them, the delineation of subunits profoundly affects resource and information flows within the firm. The extent to which people have ready access to the information and resources essential to performing their jobs depends on how they are grouped. For example, many large, primarily domestic firms have responded to the challenge of globalization by creating a subunit to develop global markets for existing products. This unit researches market opportunities abroad, sets up marketing and distribution in other countries, and encourages other subunits to be more responsive to international markets. The rationale for creating a separate unit is often to make it easier for senior managers to direct resources to developing international markets. One unintentional consequence, however, is to isolate the international concerns from the mainstream business of the firm. What the international group learns about other markets, for example, is not readily communicated to the domestically focused units that are much more likely to respond to messages from their own marketing people.

This example is just one of the many specific embodiments of the long-standing debate in the organization literature about the optimal approach to delineating subunits. In particular, scholars and managers have struggled over whether "functional" or "divisional" structures are a better way to solve the coordination problem. In a functional organization, depicted in Figure 4-4, individuals are grouped according to the tasks they perform. Thus, for example, all human resources people are grouped together, as are all salespeople, all research and development people, and so on.

By contrast, in a divisional organization, the primary subunits are formed based on some business logic rather than on a functional logic. For example, divisions might be based on geography, customers, or technology. Figure 4-5 illustrates a divisional organization based on geography. As in the figure, each division may have functional subdivisions. However, the grouping by division is the dominant feature of the organization structure, and divisional lines divide functional specialists from one another.

The functional organization helps firms realize the benefits of specialization by facilitating information sharing and learning among technical specialists. Over time, the specialists become increasingly expert at performing their particular function. For example, grouping all the engineers together provides more opportunity for cross-fertilization of engineering knowledge than there would be in a divisional structure that separated engineers in each division from one another. Two manufacturing divisions, each of which makes a distinct product line, may have a common process problem involving molded plastics, for example. If one group solves the problem, the organization might benefit from having a mechanism for sharing that solution with the other division. If the engineers are grouped together, this diffusion happens easily. If the engineers are separated by product line, it will be more difficult.

A functional delineation of subgroups also promotes individual investment in learning within that functional specialty. In the typical functional design, a well-

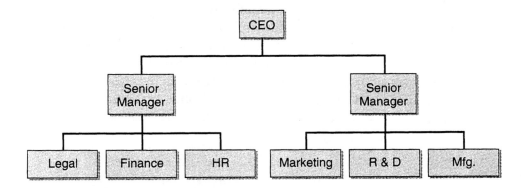

FIGURE 4-4 A Functional Architecture

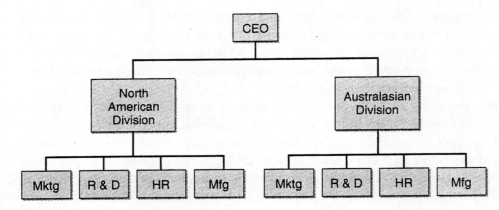

FIGURE 4-5 A Divisional Architecture

developed hierarchy within each function encourages the development and retention of the functional specialists. When the engineers are grouped together, for example, there is usually a clear engineering hierarchy, and the positions in it are well-defined stepping stones along a career path. Since the route to advancement within the function is clear, employees are motivated to specialize and invest in the human capital necessary to advance within the hierarchy. In a divisional structure, by contrast, the route to advancing one's career is typically less clear and may not be best approached by investing in function-specific skills.[5]

Despite these advantages of a functional organization, the divisional form has become increasingly common primarily because it is better at facilitating coordination *across* functions. If they are in the same subunit, those responsible for design and manufacturing are likely to learn more quickly about changes in customer tastes from the sales force than they would in a functional organization. In functional organizations, sales and marketing personnel may find themselves making unrealistic commitments to customers because they are unaware of the constraints in the design and production process. The divisional form is superior to the functional form at facilitating the coordination of different functions because it is designed precisely to accomplish this.

The value of the divisional approach increases as the firm increases in scale and scope. As the business historian Alfred Chandler has shown, the multidivisional form arose early in the twentieth century in the United States because the functional form was not well suited to the size and scope of industrial enterprises such as General Electric and DuPont. According to Chandler, improvements in the transportation and communication infrastructure and increasingly efficient capital markets made it possible and desirable for firms to grow into large and diverse commercial enterprises. As the enterprises grew in size and complexity, however, a general loss of accountability

---

[5] One can move to positions with responsibility for a more important region, a more profitable product, or a more prestigious customer. However, even if divisions can be ranked by prominence within the firm, there is still much less clarity about how career paths unfold through those divisions.

and a breakdown in communication occurred. Segmenting the activities of the firm according to divisions rather than functions, Chandler claims, enhanced accountability and communication.[6]

Regardless of how an organization resolves the functional versus divisional debate, some resources and information must cross group boundaries. One of the roles played by the senior managers overseeing multiple subunits is to function as an overarching governance structure that can communicate information and share resources among groups. Communication with and among senior managers is one way to coordinate the actions of the subunits. This process, however, requires that information collected by the subunits be passed up through the hierarchy, evaluated by senior managers, and addressed by commands and resources passed down through the hierarchy. How effectively this process accomplishes coordination is affected by how "flat" or "tall" the hierarchy is, that is, how many layers the organization structure has. Smaller, more focused firms tend to have flatter hierarchies. As the firm grows, it adds employees, and to keep the number of employees supervised by one person from growing too large, it tends to add layers to its hierarchy. At one time, General Electric had as many as nine layers of management! In flat organization structures, a request for cooperation need only "go up" the hierarchy a few steps before it reaches someone who can authorize the necessary interaction among groups.

However flat the structure, information is inevitably lost as it moves across formal boundaries. The CEO of IBM once purportedly complained that every time reports moved up another step in the hierarchy, 20 percent of the bad news was filtered out. By the time information reached the CEO, it was all good news. Passing information along consumes resources, causes delays, and degrades the information by introducing noise and distortion. This cost of passing along information is the rationale for allocating decision-making rights to those with the most immediate access to the relevant information. If the marketing group for a product is given broad discretion to set prices, it can respond quickly and appropriately to the information it gets from its customers.

The problem of pushing decision making down the hierarchy is that those closest to customers, for example, may not have vital pieces of information that others who are further removed possess. In particular, they may not know how their decisions will affect other subunits. Hewlett-Packard, for example, has separate subunits for desktop printers and the replaceable ink cartridges for them. Those in the printer group may fail to take into account that the prices they charge for printers affect demand for replacement cartridges and vice versa. Recognizing this problem, the managers to whom both groups report might want either to make these decisions themselves or to create other formal linking mechanisms that will allow the decisions to be coordinated.

The assignment of decision rights, then, and the flow of information must be closely linked. One basic principle of organization design is to assign authority to

---

[6] Alfred Chandler, *Scale and Scope* (Cambridge, MA: Harvard University Press, 1990).

those who have information. If information is largely decentralized within the organization, a strong argument can be made for decentralizing decision making as well. The countervailing force is the need for closely coordinated action that argues for centralized decision making accompanied by linkages that are effective at transmitting information up through the hierarchy. Typically, it is possible to decentralize decisions that require little coordination and to centralize authority for those decisions that require more coordination.

An alternative approach to resorting to hierarchy for achieving coordination is to rely on horizontal linkages. Horizontal linking mechanisms facilitate information and resource flows without affecting the organization of the subunits. Thus, an appropriate linking mechanism may allow for some cooperation across units without sacrificing the gains from specialization and decentralization. For example, a firm can use a functional structure to facilitate technical excellence within each function and still achieve some cross-functional sharing of information or knowledge.

Examples of Horizontal Linkages

Horizontal linkages can be created in many ways, as can be illustrated with some examples. Those at the top of this list are generally less costly in the sense that they require less formally allocated time and resources. Those at the bottom of the list, however, are more formal and robust in that they can create effective linkages even when the boundaries of the subunits are difficult to cross. In formal organizations where lines of control and communication are rigidly followed, accomplishing effective coordination through horizontal linkages that cut across the hierarchy is difficult. In these circumstances, a more formal horizontal linkage may be necessary.

- **Personal networks.** Personal networks can be effective conduits for resources and information. They do not have to be established by management, but instead may arise through the actions of individual employees to meet particular needs. This characteristic is particularly valuable in a volatile environment where management may have limited insight into which linkages would be useful. However, relying on personal networks has some drawbacks. First, in a large, complex organization, individuals may not be aware of all the potential sources of information or resources. Second, these networks have no formal authority; no individual can force another to cooperate. Third, although personal networks can often be valuable for bilateral coordination, they are less effective in addressing more widespread problems that concern many groups.
- **Liaisons.** The liaison role—a formally designated linkage between units— may be useful when managers can identify a need for an intergroup linkage that personal networks are unlikely to support. FCB-Publicis (a recently dissolved alliance of two advertising agencies), for example, used liaisons to link operations in different countries when serving a global client. When it had an account with a multinational firm in the United States and another account with that same firm in France and Spain, it would rely on a liaison to coordinate the country-specific operations.

- **Task forces or teams.** A task force is a group formed for a limited time to address a particular issue, frequently one that concerns multiple units. For example, suppose that a multinational organization, divided into country-specific units, has had trouble extending its markets from its commercial base into the growing public sectors. Senior management might form a task force devoted to this topic that would assimilate and disseminate information across units. Unlike a liaison role, a task force generally has some formal authority to implement its conclusions, or it reports directly to someone who does have that authority. Teams are similar to task forces in scope but tend to have a more open-ended duration. So a firm may use a team to address issues that are of ongoing concern to several organizational units. For example, management in a multidivisional organization might create a cross-divisional manufacturing team to track and disseminate information on best practice in manufacturing processes. Like task forces, teams generally are removed from day-to-day workflow.
- **"Integrators."** Integrators also have some formal authority but are usually more closely intertwined with day-to-day operations than either task forces or teams. For example, Novo-Nordisk, a Danish pharmaceutical and chemical firm, relies on a 14-person team of "facilitators" to transfer best practice among and evaluate the performance of, approximately 300 units within the company. Over a three-year period, facilitators meet with each unit, help set performance goals, and provide information about practices observed in other units that the unit they are meeting with might find useful. A facilitator must have a wide range of contacts within the firm, share the perspectives of the groups with whom he works, and be able to exercise influence on the basis of technical expertise. So, for instance, at Novo-Nordisk, the facilitators are recruited from a broad cross-section of both staff and line functions. With each unit they evaluate, their experience and knowledge grow, further enhancing their ability to play the integrating role.

Interdependence among subunits is a key factor in selecting among the options for linking them. As an example of largely independent subunits, consider an oil firm that is also diversified into products unrelated to petroleum. It is unlikely that the activities in the petroleum divisions will affect the outcomes of activities undertaken by employees in the other divisions.[7] At the other extreme, divisions engaged in designing a system may be very interdependent. In engine design, for example, a change in the size, cost, energy requirements, physical location, or durability of one component can have significant implications for the design (and designers) of other components. As a consequence, there is a lot of interdependence among those who design different parts of the car. To allow the organization to respond effectively to

---

[7] Whenever units are part of the same firm, they have *some* interdependence. A bad year for one unit, for example, may affect the resources the firm makes available to another. When the price of oil plummeted in 1986, oil companies reduced their investment in nonoil businesses in response to the cash-flow constraint created by poor performance in the oil divisions (see Owen Lamont "Cash Flow and Investment: Evidence from Internal Capital Markets," *The Journal of Finance* 52, No. 1, (February 1997), pp. 83–109).

this kind of technological interdependence, an automobile firm's organization design will have a subunit structure and linking mechanisms that facilitate complex and frequent interconnections. We use the term "tightly coupled" to refer to organization designs with those characteristics. A more "loosely coupled" design is appropriate when the units really are largely independent or when the interface between them is standardized. Indeed, some interfaces are so standardized that assemblers can buy components off the shelf; the component designers are so loosely coupled that they are not even part of the same firm!

So far, we have limited our discussion of the organization's structure to solving the coordination problem, but architectural structure can also respond to the incentive problem. For example, the extent to which hidden action and hidden information exist within the unit depends on how the unit is defined. The incentive problem for a unit that is distinct from other units and has its own profit and loss reporting is more easily solved than it is when a unit's performance is difficult to evaluate. We therefore discuss the incentive problem in greater detail and the role that compensation and rewards can play in ameliorating it. We then return to how structure can support compensation and rewards in dealing with that problem.

Architecture: Compensation and Rewards

One of the primary ways our understanding of organizations has advanced in recent years is in the area of defining and solving the incentive problem. We have learned that hidden action and hidden information make it impossible to observe precisely what a unit has done and what it knew when it did it. As a result, if a firm wants its employees to behave in a way that is best for the firm, it cannot simply tell them what to do and then check to see that they did it.

Fortunately, a firm can sometimes *induce* the behavior it desires by creating the proper incentives. Financial incentives tied to the performance of the unit are often a powerful instrument for inducing profit-maximizing behavior. For example, consider a setting in which the members of the unit are highly motivated by financial rewards and in which the firm can easily measure what a unit contributes to the firm's profit. In this situation, the firm can align the actions of the unit fairly closely with the firm's goals by tying the compensation of the unit's managers to the unit's profit contribution. This approach to inducing people to take the actions the firm wants them to take is now commonly used. Firms with separate divisions frequently give each division its own profit and loss accountability and tie the compensation of division managers to divisional performance.

Although tying pay to profitability will, in principle, solve the incentive problem, certain problems limit how effective such plans are in practice. For example, these types of compensation schemes can lead to substantial variation in compensation over time. The same hard work might produce more profit when the macroeconomic climate is good than when it is bad. If employees are risk averse, they are either unwilling to bear this risk or must at least be compensated for doing so.

Moreover, it is often difficult to ascertain the profit impact of a unit's activities. For example, a product design unit does not generate profits on its own. One possible solution to this problem is to tie the compensation of the unit's manager to the profit of the whole firm rather than to that of the unit. However, that tends to result in weak incentives for most employees. For example, consider a large firm like Asea Brown Boveri (ABB), a European firm that designs and manufactures large-scale power generation equipment and has over 200,000 employees in over 140 countries. A manager of a design group for a single system knows that her unit might be able to contribute some amount to firm productivity. But she also knows that whatever contribution the subunit makes will be swamped by the combined contribution of the other units and—possibly—by changes in the market context. So realizing any return on the unit's hard work is uncertain. Indeed, the subunit's payment might not be affected by how hard it works. Furthermore, even if its contribution does lead to an overall profit increase, the employees in the unit will share the reward with the 200,000 other employees in the company. At best, the unit will get only a small share of any profit increment it can generate.

This argument is relevant for all employees in the organization unless they are members of the firm's top management. The most senior members of the firm recognize that their impact on firm performance can be large enough to survive the combined actions of other employees and the environment. Furthermore, since there are only a few top managers, they can expect to get a larger share of the profit increment for which they are responsible. This is why one sees large option grants and other forms of contingent compensation offered to CEOs and other members of the top management team and less incentive pay for those further down in the hierarchy.

Because tying compensation to *overall* firm profits doesn't provide much incentive to act as the firm would like (at least for most of its workers) and the profit contribution of the subunit can be difficult to measure, firms typically tie compensation to some combination of imperfect indicators of unit performance. For example, firms have used the results of customer satisfaction surveys, the owner's assessment of how hard everyone seems to be working when she stops by the firm for a surprise visit, the number of patents awarded, meeting time-to-market schedules, and so forth. In deciding which indicators might be best, the senior managers must use their knowledge of the organization, including the nature of the tasks performed by a subunit, the information available, and the cost of monitoring.

In selecting indicators, managers can follow four rules of thumb. First, as one would expect, indicators that are highly correlated with the direct profit impact of the unit's work are more useful than indicators that are only weakly correlated with it. Thus the profitability of ABB in the country served by a design unit is a better indicator than the worldwide performance of ABB because the group has more effect on ABB's profitability in that country than on ABB's overall profitability. Note that it is profit impact that one wants to be correlated with the indicator; managers want to avoid indicators that can be manipulated without affecting the firm's profit. A medical laboratory, for example, once set up an incentive scheme that made technician pay sensitive to the variance in lab test turnaround times. The idea was to be able to give customers a reliable estimate of how long it would take to get lab test results. The effect was that the technicians dramatically reduced the variance in duration by holding up results that otherwise would have been available much earlier than others. Average turnaround time increased!

Second, it is useful to have indicators that allow one to "net out" the effects of factors beyond the control of the unit. For example, if the country goes into an economic decline, the firm does not want to punish the design unit for the sales decline. More generally, many elements contribute to a unit's performance that have little to do with the unit's actions and for which, therefore, the unit should not be rewarded or punished. Benchmarking the unit's performance against other units or firms that face many of the same challenges is one way to address this problem. Relative performance is frequently used, for example, in evaluating the performance of senior managers. The board of directors should ask how well the firm has done relative to its competitors. Using the performance of other firms has the advantage of responding to the hidden information problem. If a unit's performance is evaluated based on its own reports of the economic conditions it faced, the unit has an incentive to exaggerate its difficulties.

Third, since no one indicator tells you exactly what you want to know, there is a benefit to including several indicators in the incentive scheme. We have already suggested, for example, that managers should consider both the profit generated by the unit and factors that might affect that profit but are beyond the control of the unit. This means that the indicators should include some measure(s) of profit and some measure(s) of factors external to the unit that might affect its profits. More generally, including multiple dimensions minimizes the effect of errors in any one indicator. For example, a manager's assessment of a design unit's contribution might be one of the best indicators of performance available. But, like all indicators, it will be imperfect. More specifically, it will be "noisy" and it might be "biased." "Bias" means that the assessment is systematically wrong. The manager may simply like the head of the unit and therefore give it higher marks than it deserves, for example. "Noise" means the assessment is imprecise, but it is as likely to be too favorable as it is to be too harsh. Even if the alternative indicators available are less good (i.e., have more noise or bias), including additional indicators improves the combined information. The idea is similar to the benefits of forming a stock market portfolio in preference to investing in a single, even high-quality, stock. A portfolio can eliminate idiosyncratic risk, creating a return that is a good indicator of the health of the economy.

There is, of course, a limit to the number of indicators one wants to use. One reason for this is that information collection is costly, an issue we return to below. Another is that as the number of indicators used rises, the people in the unit may find it increasingly difficult to anticipate how the overall score is affected by what they do. When there are many indicators, no single one seems to count much toward the performance evaluation. If employees have little incentive to attend to any particular criterion, the incentive effects of the entire package will be negligible. This concern casts doubt on the efficacy of the increasingly popular "balanced scorecard" approach in which employees are rated according to a large array of indicators.

Finally, managers should consider the cost of monitoring. Some indicators may allow an accurate assessment of the unit's performance but be extremely costly to administer. The so-called 360 degree evaluation schemes—in which an individual employee is evaluated by superiors, peers, subordinates, and often key external constituencies as well—can provide refined information on individual performance but are extremely time-consuming. Constructing more accurate measures makes it easier to reward the "right" behavior and therefore will induce employees to take the actions the firm desires. But the cost of collecting the information might offset the gain. Information collected through an extremely detailed cost accounting procedure might be useful in providing incentives, for example, but the cost of collecting the data and doing the required analysis may be greater than the increase in revenues created by getting more of the desired behavior.

The problem of finding indicators that are informative is particularly severe for effort that involves cooperation among subunits. We alluded to this problem earlier when we commented that the design group typically does not have profit and loss responsibility because the value of its output is hard to disentangle from the value provided by manufacturing and distribution. Suppose the product is wildly successful. Who should get credit for the profits it generates? The basic problem is that there are generally few good indicators of the value each subunit contributes to the overall outcome even when that can be easily valued. One way firms try to solve this problem is by establishing transfer prices that are benchmarked to market prices. Often, however, there are no market prices because what is exchanged has no market counterpart. It is hard to know what the value of a particular design might be. Furthermore, much cooperative effort involves the exchange of information. This is difficult both to value and to track.

The firm's problem is complicated because the mechanisms put in place to get the subunit to be productive on its own may give it an incentive to avoid cooperation. Investment banks, for example, are notorious for building high-powered incentives for individual traders. More than half a trader's income, for example, is often in the form of a bonus for individual performance. Since a person can work no more than 24 hours a day, someone whose pay is so strongly tied to his own performance faces a huge incentive to avoid spending any time helping other workers. The opportunity cost of diverting time to cooperation is just too high. If the pay-for-performance scheme also involves a relative performance component so that top performers within the firm are disproportionately rewarded, a trader may even have an incentive to devote some time to impairing the performance of his co-workers.

Earlier, we mentioned that architectural structure can also affect the incentive problem. One way it can do so is by affecting the importance of cooperation across units. Consider, for example, a firm's decision about whether to market its products under a single brand or under multiple brands. Some firms, like 3M, Sony, IBM, Nike, or Xerox, build the brand name at the level of the firm, prominently attaching the name of the firm to many of its products. Other firms, like Procter & Gamble, PepsiCo, or Johnson & Johnson, build brands around individual products, segments, or divisions. Finally, others adopt a mixed approach to branding. In Europe, Daimler-Benz uses the Mercedes brand for both cars and trucks. In the United States, Daimler-Benz adopts a multibrand strategy, producing passenger cars under the Mercedes name and commercial trucks under the Freightliner and Sterling brands.

Although marketing concerns usually drive this branding decision, it has less obvious, but important, organizational implications. If a brand cuts across two separate organizational units, the identities and performances of the two units are intertwined. The decision of one unit to offer an inferior product has negative consequences for the other unit. Conversely, if one unit can improve its product, its actions create positive effects for the other. The upside of linking identities is that each unit now has a self-interested reason to assist the other; a failure to provide assistance can directly harm the unit's own performance by damaging the common brand. However, this linking also has a clear downside. Because the overall perception of the brand is a result of the aggregate effort of both subunits, neither realizes the full benefits or bears the full cost of its actions. As a result, even when the managers of each subunit are rewarded based on the performance of their own unit, neither manager has the right incentives to devote resources to supporting the common brand name. Contrast this situation with a firm in which each subunit has its own brand. Each manager has the right incentives to support her brand because the brand has no value for other units, and she is rewarded based on her subunit's performance. Although a common brand induces more cooperation, it also dilutes the incentives for individual performance.

Achieving high levels of cooperation will not be equally important for all organizations. One reason an investment bank has high-powered incentives for individual performance is that its profit is affected more by the aggregate of individual performance than it is by the level of cooperation among its units. Many other firms depend much more on cooperation among subunits. A firm for which innovation is critical, for example, tends to stress cooperation more. This is in part because rewarding individual performance is harder for this kind of firm. It is harder to tie firm performance to a specific unit's R&D performance, and the returns to any unit's initiative are so variable that tying compensation to them would lead to large variance in compensation over time. Equally important, however, the success of the R&D units often depends on cooperation with other units within the firm.

The difficulty of inducing cooperative behavior with strong financial incentives or carefully drawn organizational boundaries underscores the importance of other elements of organization design in solving the incentive problem. The focus here is on compensation schemes and boundaries because they are powerful tools and can be manipulated much more easily than many other elements of organization design. They clearly are not a panacea for the incentive problem, however, and managers should recognize that other elements can also be brought to bear on the problem. Recognizing the limits of architecture, we now turn to the contributions of routines and culture.

Routines

Much of the day-to-day activity and decision making within a firm are accomplished through the exercise of routines. As a simple example, consider a firm's routines for repairing its products. A customer's call about a problem is routed to the repair department. Often, someone responsible for "triage" will determine the precise nature of the problem and route the call to a qualified repair person. If the expert cannot resolve the problem over the phone, the customer will be told how to return the product. When the product is returned, it is routed to the appropriate repair personnel. After making the repair, these people route the paperwork to the warranty department and the repaired product to shipping. Each of the people involved in this process understands the circumstances that require them to act, the tasks for which they are responsible, and how to hand off specific tasks for which they do not have responsibility.

The key to routines is that they embody established *interfaces* among the parties that must interact in the performance of a process. The interfaces consist of common expectations about what will flow across them and a protocol for accomplishing the transfer. The shipping department knows that it will receive parts and the paperwork that tells it where the part should be shipped. On an assembly line, each worker knows what subassembly should be arriving at her workstation and how it will arrive. Having finished her work, she knows how the subassembly should pass to the next set of actors.

There are large coordination gains to this kind of routinization. Each employee can become expert at some subprocess. The shipping department, for example, gets good at packaging and handling the interactions with various common carriers because this is all that it does. Routines, therefore, support the realization of gains from specialization. Perhaps more importantly, because interfaces are standardized, there are huge informational efficiencies. As tasks proceed from one unit to another, only minimal amounts of information need be communicated between units. Each unit need know only what is essential for it to play its part, including how to interpret the information it receives and transmit the information necessary for the next step to the next unit.

Importantly, routines do not just apply to linear processes of the kind illustrated by the repair example. Firms also have routines for decision making, for example. In some organizations, group decisions are generally made by consensus. Strong opposition from even one person within a group can prevent the group from pursuing a particular plan. Other organizations make decisions by majority rule. Still others have some implicit weighting scheme based on rank, seniority, or expertise. Most organizations do not reevaluate these decision rules every time a decision is made. Rather, the organization has a decision routine that it applies each time a decision must be made.

Since many routines cross group boundaries, they facilitate coordination among groups by simplifying the interface. A routine way for employees in one division to access the resources in another division enables the firm to coordinate in ways that would be difficult if the firm had to make a new resource-sharing decision each time. Routines, once taken for granted, may obviate the need for structural linking mechanisms or intervention by managers. Moreover, in contrast to linking processes that function well for infrequent coordination, routines are excellent devices for repeated coordination because they develop from and rely on repetition.

Routines also ameliorate the incentive problem. First, they create opportunities to get better indicators of performance. Standardized interfaces make standardized indicators possible. In our repair example, the triage person can easily record referrals to repair people in a database. Similarly, shipping can record when the repaired part is received for shipment, and the warranty department can record when the warranty information is received. Routines also ameliorate incentive problems by "automating" activities for which it is otherwise difficult to provide incentives. By standardizing the interfaces among units, routines facilitate cooperation.

Culture

The commonly held values and beliefs of an organization both constrain and enable the actions firms can take. Employees regard a decision they perceive to be consistent with common values and beliefs as substantively appropriate and worthy of support. Similarly, they view a decision-making process as procedurally just if they believe it conforms to the sanctioned criteria, even when they dislike the outcome. The converse, of course, is also true. Members of the organization will resist any course of action that appears to violate the culture of the firm.

Culture, then, provides the opportunity for inducing cooperation that otherwise would be difficult to achieve. Subunits are generally reluctant to give up resources, especially when they have difficulty understanding how those resources might be applied elsewhere. A culture that promotes communication and resource sharing can economize on the hierarchy and structural linking mechanisms necessary to accomplish resource and information sharing. Cooperation is particularly likely if there is a well-developed "norm of reciprocity": the belief that one is obligated to help those who have helped oneself.

Many companies consciously combine financial incentives and culture to elicit a balance of individual performance and cooperation. Hewlett-Packard (HP), for example, creates strong financial incentives at the divisional level by assigning profit and loss responsibility to divisions and, with few exceptions, does not allow one division to subsidize another. If a division cannot generate a profit on its own, it effectively dies. Given these strong division-level incentives, one would expect to see limited cooperation across divisions. The strong financial incentives for individual divisions, however, are balanced by a corporate culture that fosters interdivisional cooperation. Because this culture is important, HP has made it as explicit as possible, describing it as "The HP Way." HP's statement of its corporate objectives begins: "The achievements of an organization are the result of the combined efforts of each individual in the organization working toward common objectives. These objectives should be realistic, should be clearly understood by everyone in the organization and should reflect the organization's basic character and personality."[8]

Common beliefs about the firm and its external context also can help employees focus on those tasks that are important for the competitive advantage of the firm. Southwest Airlines' strategy requires its employees to pay attention to customers. If employees believe that this is necessary for the firm to succeed, they are more likely to regard dancing in the aisles as reasonable behavior. Furthermore, one of the reasons employees at Southwest trust senior managers to make the right decisions is that employees and managers have a common view of the world. Another is that Southwest has created an implicit contract with its employees that it will treat them fairly, con-

---

[8] You can find this statement and a description of "The HP Way" on their Web site www.hp.com/abouthp/hpway.html, accessed March 2000.

sider their perspective, and be responsive to their views of how the organization should change.

Culture can also play a vital role in resolving the foundation of the incentive problem. Recall that our discussion of incentives is premised on the notion that the firm and subordinate unit (or individuals) have different goals. However, suppose that this were not true; suppose that the firm and subunit have the same objectives. Then, management need not worry about offering incentives to the unit to pursue the firm's goals because the unit *wants* to pursue those goals. One view of culture is that it affects what people want to do *in the absence of pecuniary* rewards. Suppose, for example, that the competitive advantage of an organization hinges on innovation and product quality. If the employees derive considerable satisfaction from developing and being associated with high-quality products, then the firm has less need to offer financial incentives for this behavior. A manager who wants to induce a particular behavior that is difficult or costly to include in a pay-for-performance scheme may find that a strong culture can be a more effective means of evoking that particular behavior than pecuniary incentives.

4.6 ARC ANALYSIS

In this chapter, we have introduced some of the key concepts of organization design and developed a framework for approaching the complex problem of building a high-performance organization. We summarize that framework in Figure 4-6 under the label *ARC Analysis*. As illustrated in the figure, any effective design must address two general problems: *coordinating* the deployment of the firm's assets and aligning the *incentives* of its employees and units with those of the firm. The managers charged with designing the organization have three organizational levers to tackle these problems: *architecture, routines,* and *culture* (ARC). As indicated by the arrows connecting them in the figure, these levers interact, and an effective design depends on the three elements of ARC working in concert. We also noted that the coordination and incen-

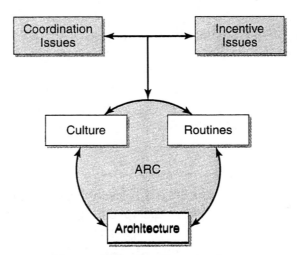

FIGURE 4-6 ARC Analysis: Building an Effective Organization

tive problems are intertwined. The way the coordination problem is solved, for example, affects the incentive problems the design must resolve. The bidirectional arrow between these problems in the figure is meant to represent this interdependence.

This framework suggests that managers must have a deep understanding of the elements of the firm's ARC, how those elements fit together, and how they address the firm's incentive and coordination problem. This is easy advice to give, but, as we have seen throughout the chapter, it is difficult to follow. Because organization design has many elements with intricate relationships among them, it poses formidable problems. The complexity that makes organization design difficult, however, also means that getting it right can create a competitive advantage that is difficult for others to match.

One way to approach this problem is to have a systematic approach to collecting information on the design challenge facing the firm and the elements of its architecture, culture, and routines. In Figure 4-7 we have listed some of the questions that managers who want to collect and evaluate this kind of information might usefully pose (and answer!). In Part A, we present some of the questions that are helpful for thinking through what kind of design problems the firm faces. This is the "green field" part of the problem. The idea here is to step back from the existing organization and ask what the firm needs to do (its coordination problem) and how its employees and units will be motivated to do it (the incentive problem). It is "green field" because it ignores the existing organization of the firm. It does not ask what problems the current organization addresses or fails to address, but what problems would be addressed if management could build an entirely new organization. As we shall see in the next chapter, defining these questions and arriving at answers are intimately tied to the firm's strategy. It is the strategy that determines the central design issues for the firm.

Part B of the figure brings us back to the current organization of the firm. The questions illustrated here are those that enable the managers to conduct a detailed analysis of the firm's current ARC. The answers to the questions posed in this stage should produce a rich description of the firm's structure, compensation and reward systems, routines, and culture. Once this description is complete, the manager is in a good position to identify any inconsistencies among the elements that make the organization less effective than it could be. Now the manager also has the information to ask whether the organization as it is currently designed is responsive to the key coordination and incentive problems it needs to solve. Laying out the details of the organization is a necessary step to understanding what parts of its design are appropriate and what parts should be reconsidered.

4.7 SUMMARY

A firm's competitive advantage often has its basis in the firm's organization. An effective organization design must address the specific coordination and incentive problems the firm faces and must do so in a way that supports the firm's strategy. The components of organization design that a firm can manipulate to address its coordination and incentive problems are its architecture, routines, and culture (ARC). The

Part A: Defining the Problem

Coordination Problem
- How does critical information reach the firm?
- How should information flow through the firm?
- Who should make which decisions?
- What activities should be grouped together?
- What cross-unit linkages should be created?
- What activities should be routinized?
- What norms and decision rules should be supported?
- What beliefs about the firm and its environment are important?

Incentive Problem
- What activities are most critical to the performance of the firm?
- What performance dimensions can be measured and monitored?
- Where will incentive pay be most effective?
- What kind of culture will support productive behavior?
- What hiring and performance review routines are appropriate?

Part B: Assessing the Firm's Response

Architecture			
Structure	Compensation and Rewards	Routines	Culture
• Is the structure divisional or functional? • How is it divided into subunits? • What formal linking mechanisms exist? 　• Personal networks? 　• Liaisons? 　• Task forces? 　• Integrators? • How interdependent are subunits? • How frequently are they interdependent? • What structures exist for resource allocation? • What structures exist for sharing information? • How tall/flat is the hierarchy? • Where and how are decision rights allocated?	• How high is compensation relative to other firms in the industry? • How important are nonfinancial elements of compensation? • How important is incentive compensation? • How closely is compensation tied to performance of the unit? • How is performance measured? • Does compensation depend on impact on other units? If so, how is that measured? • How important and prevalent is promotion from within?	• What routines exist for resource allocation? • What routines exist for sharing information among subunits? • What routines exist for coordinating across boundaries between subunits? • What routines exist for coordinating activity within subunits? • What routines exist that give senior management visibility into what is happening at lower levels? • What interfaces exist that facilitate the use of routines? • How are the interfaces defined? maintained? What is the process for ensuring routines survive over time and are disseminated across the organization?	• How strong is the culture? • What are its key characteristics? • What norms support the culture? • What "stories" are key to the maintenance of the culture? • Does the culture support cooperation across units? • Does the culture reduce the need for financial incentives to induce cooperation? • Do the firms' recruitment policies reinforce the culture?

FIGURE 4-7 ARC Analysis Questions

framework developed here is helpful for creating an internally consistent ARC that effectively addresses the incentive and coordination problems the firm faces.

The framework developed in this chapter only brings us part way, however, to answering the basic question with which we began this chapter: How does the internal context of the firm determine its competitive advantage? Put differently, how does the manager know what the key incentive and coordination problems are for her firm? We asserted that these are determined by the firm's strategy, but we have not directly addressed how this connection works. In the next chapter we turn to thinking through the linkage between strategy and organization design.

CHAPTER

5

ORGANIZATION AND COMPETITIVE ADVANTAGE

5.1 INTRODUCTION

A manager is concerned with organization because it affects the success of the firm's strategy. We have argued that a strategy should contain a set of objectives, a statement of scope, a clearly stated competitive advantage, and logic that explains how the internal context of the firm will enable it to achieve its objectives given its external context. In Chapter 4 we developed tools that allow us to think systematically about organization design. In this chapter we focus on the logic that connects that organization design with competitive advantage. The central question here is: "Is the firm organized to support the competitive advantage it needs to achieve its objectives?" To answer this question, the firm's managers must first understand the specific organization design problems implied by its strategy. Once the firm's managers have identified what specific coordination and incentive issues are implicit in the strategy they are pursuing, they can build an appropriate architecture, routines, and culture (ARC).

Alignment between strategy and organization is critical to meeting the firm's strategic objectives. A high-service retailer like Harrod's should be organized differently from one that focuses on low costs such as Kmart. The organization of a firm like the game company, Sega, whose strategy hinges on rapid time-to-market, should be different from that of a steel company whose product development cycle is considerably slower and whose customers care more about reliability and price than innovation. Because organization and strategy are interdependent, we need, and in the next section will develop, a conceptual framework for exploring the relationship between strategy and organization.

Although this framework helps ensure that the organization "fits" the strategy, we also need to recognize that the relationship between a firm's organization and its competitive advantage changes over time. As the firm seeks to deepen its current advantage or build new competitive advantage, it has to change the way it deploys its resources. The firm must create an organization that supports the changes it needs to make. In section 5.3 we discuss two different approaches to organization design that enable a firm to meet this challenge. One design is particularly suitable for a firm intent on creating the continual and incremental change necessary to maintain its existing competitive advantage. Firms with this design and intent are called "exploiters" because they are focused on successfully exploiting the competitive advantage they already have.

The second design type is better suited to a firm that is attempting to create a new competitive advantage either because the firm wants to change its strategic scope or because it needs to exploit new technologies. Firms that are predominantly in the business of continually creating new capabilities, for example, fall in this category. Firms organized to generate a stream of advantageous capabilities or positions are called "explorer" firms.[1]

Almost no firms are pure explorers or exploiters. Most firms need to be proficient at both exploration and exploitation to be successful over the long haul. Although successful firms typically have elements of both exploration and exploitation, the organization design requirements of each are sufficiently distinct that it is difficult for the same firm to be equally good at both exploring and exploiting. Indeed, most managers can readily identify whether their firm is better equipped to explore or exploit. It is then a short step to evaluating whether the explorer-exploiter mix the firm is pursuing fits its external environment and its strategy. It is sometimes easy to see, for example, that a firm's historical strength in exploiting its current market segment is preventing it from seeing and therefore, seizing, new strategic opportunities. Or a firm's continual preoccupation with catching the next wave of technology may blind it to the opportunities for more profitably exploiting its current technology. The language of "explorers" and "exploiters" therefore provides useful shorthand for evaluating the firm's approach to maintaining or changing its competitive advantage—shorthand that we will return to in later chapters. However, we emphasize that it is shorthand, and though useful as a conceptual device, most firms resemble neither extreme, but rather must both explore and exploit to be successful. In the last section we discuss the problem of combining exploration and exploitation.

5.2 ALIGNING STRATEGY AND ORGANIZATION

In Chapter 4, we developed the concept of ARC analysis. This framework can be used to articulate the firm's key coordination and incentive problems and to assess whether its ARC effectively addresses those challenges. However, a firm can have a consistent and elegant solution to a set of coordination and incentive problems and still have a woefully inadequate design from a strategic perspective. The design must not only "work," it must do the work that is necessary to achieve the firm's strategic goals. In particular, as suggested by Figure 5-1, it must fit with the competitive advantage at the center of the firm's strategy. When there is a good fit between the

---

[1] The terms, "explorer" and "exploiter" were coined by Jim March in "Exploration and Exploitation in Organizational Learning," *Organization Science*, 2, No. 1 (February 1991), 71–87.

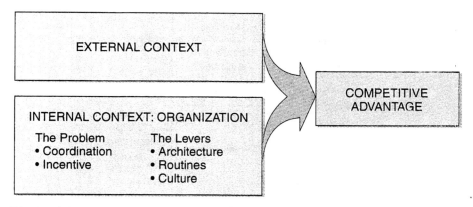

FIGURE 5-1 The Link between Internal Context and Competitive Advantage

firm's design and its competitive advantage, we say that the organization is "strategically aligned" with the strategy. Strategic alignment is a key strategy concept and our main focus in this section of the chapter.

As an example of strategic alignment, a firm with a competitive advantage of being the low-cost provider in its industry should have an ARC designed to achieve low costs. This type of firm might want to provide incentives that reward implementing cost-reducing process innovations and make the efficient flow of appropriate cost accounting information to key decision makers an important part of its coordination plan. It may also want to institute performance pay for its salespeople that rewards them for sales volumes, so that the firm can take advantage of production savings associated with large-scale manufacturing. If the firm is producing a commodity product like concrete, it may not be interested in customer feedback and need not be concerned about creating mechanisms for sales and manufacturing to exchange information with each other. By contrast, a firm with a competitive advantage based on time-to-market will want to provide incentives for timely design and to create an organization structure that features communication among marketing, design, and manufacturing groups. For this type of firm, information about cost control may be much less important than information about customer needs and about designs that are appropriate for rapid production.

Because organization design is complex, it is useful to have a framework for thinking through how strategic alignment might be accomplished. The framework we use, illustrated in Figure 5-2, combines the ARC Analysis introduced in Chapter 4 with the overall approach to understanding the determinants of firm performance discussed in Chapters 1–3.

As illustrated in Figure 5-2, we begin our analysis with a strategy that has a well-defined competitive advantage and then explore its organizational implications. This ordering should seem backwards, and indeed it completely reverses the logic in Figure 5-1. Up to now, we have largely taken the internal and external context of the firm as given and asked what performance-improving strategy a firm might develop to mitigate the problems and exploit the opportunities in that context. Here, we reverse this direction to ask a different question: If the manager has a strategy in mind that is

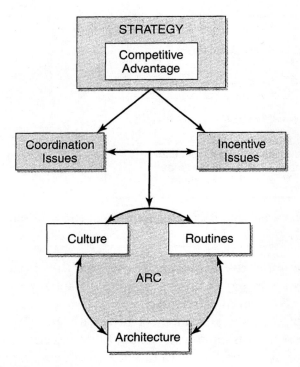

FIGURE 5-2 Strategic Alignment

appropriate for the firm's external context, what organization design will best enable the firm to carry out that strategy effectively?[2]

Given a clearly defined strategy, a manager must decide what coordination and incentive problems are most important if the firm is to achieve the competitive advantage its strategy requires. In what areas must the firm excel, and what behavior is most important if the firm is to meet its strategic objectives? In Figure 4-7, we presented a list of questions that the firm might ask about its coordination and incentive problems. An example on the coordination side is *"How does critical information reach the firm?"* Answering a question like this requires some way to assess what information is critical. Returning to our prior examples, a firm with a competitive advantage based on low cost might think information about productivity is most important, whereas a firm with a competitive advantage of time-to-market might think information about customer needs and competitor capabilities is most important. Similarly on the incentive side, how the manager responds to the question *"What kind of culture will support productive behavior?"* depends on knowing what behavior will best support the firm's competitive advantage. If sustaining volumes high enough to reap economies of scale is critical to the

---

[2] We should emphasize that we do not think strategies typically precede organization designs. Indeed, the more usual situation is that a firm exists and its managers are evaluating and refining—or even dramatically changing—its strategy. They may then turn to changing the organizational design, but it is only with new ventures that managers have the luxury of starting with a strategy and then building an organization. The diagram in Figure 5-2 is intended only to represent an analytic framework that allows a manager to explore how well the organization and strategy are aligned. We start with the firm's strategy because undertaking this exploration requires that the manager have a clear idea of what the strategy is.

firm's competitive advantage, having a culture that values salespeople who exceed quota is better than having a culture that values building close customer relationships.

The ARC of the firm is the manager's solution to the coordination and incentive problems implied by the firm's strategy. Because the optimal design depends on the strategy, there is no single "best" design. Managers can't simply impose some organizational template that will function well regardless of the competitive advantage the firm wants to pursue: They must go through a process like the one illustrated in Figure 5-2. Although the lack of a "one-size-fits-all" design requires that managers create a customized organization, starting with the imperatives of competitive advantage can also simplify the organizational design problem. Organizations are so complex that even the most diligent and creative manager will be unable to address all the design problems in her firm. Fortunately, it is not necessary to do that. What the manager must address effectively are those design problems that are most important for successfully supporting the firm's competitive advantage. This makes it essential to get certain aspects of organization right while making others less important.

Applying ARC Analysis to Assess Strategic Alignment: Southwest Airlines Revisited

To show how organization is linked to competitive advantage and what is implied by getting the key aspects of design "right," we begin by returning to the Southwest Airlines example of Chapter 4. A streamlined version of Southwest's strategy statement might read something like this: "Our strategy is to provide air service unsurpassed in customer value in selected point-to-point, short-haul markets with substantial business traffic. We deliver customer value by providing reliable, low price, customer-driven service." The competitive advantage in this statement is providing business travelers with reliable, friendly service combined with a low-cost structure that allows Southwest to offer low prices. With this strategy in mind, we can revisit the ARC analysis framework to diagnose Southwest's design.

The first step is to identify the key coordination and incentive problems implied by Southwest's strategy: combining operational efficiency with outstanding customer service. Operational efficiency means using fewer resources than its competitors to deliver the same product. Outstanding customer service means meeting the needs of its target customers better than its competitors. In the top panel of Figure 5-3, we have identified some of the specific coordination problems that might be important for Southwest. More generally, the coordination issues for this competitive advantage are to design an organization that collects and uses information on customer needs effectively while implementing mechanisms to deliver efficient service and to monitor cost and service performance. The incentive problem is to build an organization that recognizes and rewards behavior that balances cost minimization and customer service. These are also illustrated in Figure 5-3.

With the key coordination and incentive problems identified, we can review Southwest's ARC to see how Southwest addresses these problems. In the lower panel of Figure 5-3, we've summarized some of the important characteristics of Southwest's organization. At Southwest, the cross-functional team responsible for a particular

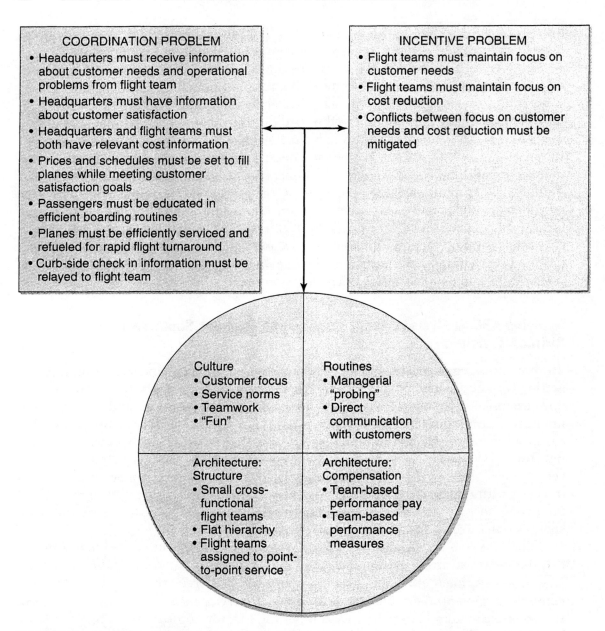

FIGURE 5-3 An Abbreviated Analysis of Southwest Airlines

route has most of the information necessary to make decisions that affect it. As a result, team members are well positioned to see and resolve problems that might delay flights. They control how quickly flights are turned around at the airport and how efficiently passengers are boarded and seated.

They also are the people who know most about the customers on that route and can make small changes to accommodate idiosyncratic problems that their frequent flyers might have. For example, a pilot has the discretion to return to the gate if a passenger has boarded the wrong plane. A culture that makes heroes of teams who provide exemplary service by any means necessary supports the efforts of these teams. When the teams encounter problems that they cannot solve, Southwest's flat hierarchy and the accessibility of its managers give them a way to ask for systemwide changes in policies or resource allocation that will enable them to perform better.

The teams also bear the cost of their decisions. The pilot who takes the plane back to the gate knows exactly what her action will mean for the flight's on-time arrival and what she and the rest of the team will have to do to make up for lost time. Any baggage handler who sees a bag going on the wrong plane can weigh the consequences of delaying the loading process by retrieving it. He also knows that his team members will support his decision because they, in turn, will count on his support when they need it.

These advantages of decentralization come at a cost to Southwest, however. Because teams make most decisions without needing to consult managers, less information about what is happening at the interface with the customer is automatically transmitted up the hierarchy. Yet it is vitally important that headquarters obtain this information if it is to disseminate best practice throughout the company and become aware of pervasive problems that need more centralized attention. Southwest attempts to improve information flows to headquarters in at least two ways. First, managers do a lot of "managing by walking around." By constantly probing throughout the firm, they can piece together a picture of what is happening lower down in the company.

Second, Southwest leverages its strong relationships with its customers to encourage direct communication with the company. Southwest responds carefully to customer letters (both of praise and complaint). For example, Southwest learned from customers' letters that a new policy allowing customers to get boarding cards when they checked in at the ticket desk rather than the gate annoyed its regular customers. Regular customers were used to being able to predict their seat assignments based on their time of arrival at the gate and could no longer do so. Southwest changed the policy. Headquarters also uses the examples of outstanding service it learns of through letters to reinforce that behavior throughout the firm by disseminating success stories to all employees.

Handling the coordination problem in this largely decentralized way also makes it fairly easy to resolve the incentive problem. Because many of the factors that determine customer satisfaction and operational efficiency are largely under the control of the local teams, it is easy to measure and provide incentives for that performance. Because team performance is easy to measure, Southwest can tie compensation to it. And because the teams are relatively small, each team member can expect to get a reasonable share of the reward. Finally, because the team members understand the contributions each member makes, it is difficult for any single member to violate the group norm. Shirking by individuals therefore is probably not a problem. While some of those incentives are financial, an advantage of the strong Southwest culture is that recognition by customers and other employees of outstanding performance is itself a reward.

In Chapter 4, we emphasized that sound organizational design requires organizational consistency. By this we mean that the firm must ensure that the entire design hangs together, with each element complementing the others and with no contradictions among them. For example, an organization designed to maximize the opportunities to learn from salespeople who are in direct contact with customers should probably have a fairly flat structure, so that few filtering layers get in the way of feedback from the salespeople to senior managers. It should complement the architecture with a culture of trust and commitment in which salespeople feel that it is important to share their ideas and in which they will not be punished for doing that. One would also expect to see routines in place that facilitate information flows, such as forums for regular contact between senior management and salespeople as well as routines for considering and acting on the feedback received.

A review of our ARC analysis for Southwest indicates that its organization design has this feature. The design combines a decentralized decision-making process with a production system in which almost all the information relevant to those decisions is readily and easily accessed by the teams. The incentive scheme that is based on team performance fits nicely with the decentralized decision making. Rewarding the teams based on the performance of the team as a unit encourages their members to support each other to maximize their own well-being. The flat hierarchy makes it easier for managers to get information by walking around and, in the process, to reinforce the culture of customer focus.

Consistent as Southwest's approach might be, it would simply not work for many of its competitors. Competitors that operate hub-and-spoke airlines cannot grant that much autonomy to the teams on specific routes. These firms also rely on product quality for competitive advantage, but their appeal is different. United Airlines, for example, delivers customer value by providing a large network of flights that allows passengers to reach many destinations without changing airlines. The value of this network is enhanced by frequent flyer programs that reward high mileage customers with free flights to many locations. Operational efficiency is achieved not by simplified, no frills service but by consolidating maintenance service at hubs and using the hub-and-spoke system to increase the number of passengers on each flight. Instead of offering a single, low fare, United offers a complex web of discounts that contributes to full flights and imposes higher costs on those travelers who are more willing to pay high prices. Implementing this kind of competitive advantage requires centralized decision making.

This is apparent in the problem of just getting planes in and out of airports on time. Airlines whose competitive advantage depends on an efficient hub-and-spoke system face the daunting task of coordinating disparate flights, all of which must arrive from and leave a hub within a short window of time. They achieve this coordination through a centralized process in which a small number of decision makers respond to exceptions with the aid of computer optimization programs. In this setting, the crews of particular flights are cogs in a much larger machine whose behavior is largely circumscribed by official policies and routines. No pilot will be called a hero for delaying a flight to accommodate a passenger who got on the wrong plane because the cost of that decision reverberates throughout the system. The hub-and-spoke operation creates a process-based interdependence among the units, which means that the coordination problem cannot be solved through decentralization. As a result, the incentive problem is also more complex.

Other Examples: Sony, Apple Computer, and Silicon Graphics

The linkages between competitive advantage and organization are not, of course, unique to airlines. In Chapter 3, for example, we mentioned that Sony has a competitive advantage based on its capability of designing consumer electronics that are small and easy to make. A firm like this is an interesting contrast to one like Apple Computer whose strategy has depended on being quick to market with cutting-edge technology. A company like Apple may be willing to accept higher manufacturing cost if that buys it performance, a tradeoff that Sony would not make. These differences in focus are particularly interesting because Apple and Sony have collaborated on projects (such as some of Apple's Powerbook laptop computers), and differences in the way they are organized have led to conflicts within these cooperative ventures.[3]

Sony's miniaturization capability hinges on a set of well-defined and well-understood engineering processes that go beyond the design and development of any particular project. Sony engineers understand that once a component (e.g., a battery) has been allocated a particular space within the product (e.g., a camcorder), that space allocation is no longer negotiable. When Apple entered into a joint venture with Sony and tried to incorporate this decision-rule into the design process for its own laptop computer, Apple's managers found that it did not fit with Apple's culture, which tolerated almost any last-minute change if it led to a more "insanely great" product. Let's assume, for the sake of argument, that the ARC of each of these firms is organizationally consistent and aligned with its distinctive competitive advantage. The problems these firms had in working together successfully underscore the importance of organizational design for performance. It was difficult for Sony to allow for the kind of design changes Apple wanted to make and still perform in a manner consistent with its competitive advantage. Similarly, Apple engineers were unable to get some of the design features they felt made Apple products so appealing to its customers when they were forced to adhere to the design-process guidelines Sony imposed.

Similarly, a company whose competitive advantage depends, at least in part, on rapid time-to-market must adapt its routines to that strategy. Silicon Graphics, for example, has attempted to compete by being the first to market with state-of-the-art technology in high-end computer workstations. Pursuing this form of competitive advantage creates a tension for the design engineers. Being state-of-the-art requires being flexible about technology because the firm needs to incorporate the most current developments in every product. On the other hand, being first to market requires efficient manufacturing. Unfortunately, efficient manufacturing is often at odds with being flexible enough to incorporate the latest technology. Consequently, Silicon Graphics was forced to create routines and linkages between design and manufacturing to coordinate activity, so that designs did not need to be "frozen" until late in the design process, but once "frozen" could be quickly manufactured.

---

[3] See Saloner, Garth, and Hank Chesbrough, "Apple Computer in the Portable Computer Market (A) and (B)," Stanford Business School, S-SM-1 and S-SM-2, April 1992.

5.3 BUILDING AND CREATING COMPETITIVE ADVANTAGE

The framework summarized in Figure 5-2 works well when the firm's competitive advantage is clearly defined and the firm has or can readily acquire the resources necessary to pursue it. But achieving competitive advantage is not a static goal. Even if the firm's strategy doesn't change, the behavior of its competitors usually forces it to refine and deepen its competitive advantage. A low-cost firm today will not be low cost tomorrow unless it can continually improve its production and distribution processes to stay one step ahead of competitors. Wal-Mart's computerized supply chain management system was a huge competitive advantage when it pioneered this kind of system. These systems, however, are now more widely used, and Wal-Mart has had to improve its system and its other supply chain management processes to retain a cost advantage.

As a firm's environment changes or as it becomes aware of new opportunities, it may also want to create new forms of competitive advantage. Sometimes the change is forced on the firm by evolution within its industry or by changes elsewhere in the economy. Sometimes the change is created within the firm as it discovers a way to serve customers it had not reached before, or new channels for distributing its goods, or new technologies that allow it to fundamentally change its product offerings. We want to focus on the organizational implications of such changes in competitive advantage. Our shift in focus is illustrated in Figure 5-4, where we reproduce Figure 5-2 with the addition of arrows flowing from ARC back to competitive advantage.

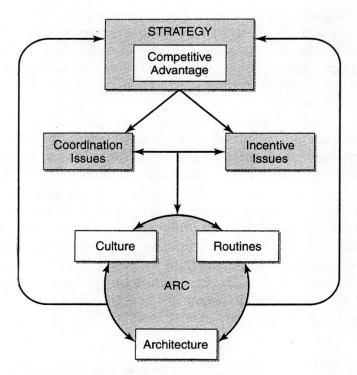

FIGURE 5-4 Strategic Alignment Implications

As the examples suggest, competitive advantage is dynamic in two senses. First, firms must continually develop and deepen current advantage if they are to meet the challenge of competition. Second, over time the firm may want to alter its strategy to pursue some other form of competitive advantage. As we stated in the introduction, we refer to the first kind of activity as "exploiting" a competitive advantage and the second as "exploring" new competitive advantages. Although every firm must engage in both of these activities, the extent to which a firm emphasizes one or the other varies. There are firms whose approach more closely resembles that of "exploiters," and others who are more like "explorers." Often the environment dictates which mode will be more successful. In a mature, stable industry, for example, exploitation may be more important for superior performance. In an industry buffeted by substantive technological or competitive change, more exploration might be optimal.

These two types of activities have very different organizational requirements. The ARC that supports exploitation is distinct from the ARC that supports exploration. Since the typical firm must both explore and exploit, doing both poses a big managerial challenge. Managers must find a way to incorporate two different sets of organizational demands within the same firm. To make this challenge concrete, we begin by treating the two extreme forms: pure explorers (that concentrate on developing new sources of competitive advantage) and pure exploiters (that concentrate on reinforcing current advantage). After examining the constellations of organizational design elements that are best suited to each of these types, we return to the issue of trying to pursue both in a single organization.

Explorers and Exploiters

Exploiters and explorers follow different business models. Since the exploiter model is predicated on continually improving the firm's products and how they are delivered, that approach can be described as "doing better what we already do." Exploiters have a well-defined domain in which they operate, and they focus on occupying that domain more successfully. They perform well to the extent that they can stay ahead of competitors. This is a standard approach to achieving the kind of sustainable competitive advantage discussed in Chapter 3. Firms that compete on the basis of low cost in competitive, mature industries are usually exploiter firms. Since the industry is mature, so is the technology of production in the industry, and the firms that cannot produce at the lowest possible costs cannot survive. A good exploiter is a firm that sticks to its knitting and knits well.

Explorer firms, in contrast, hope to prosper by finding completely novel ways of doing things, rather than doing the same things a little better. They worry about the needs of new customer segments, emerging market opportunities, and how to leverage the firm's resources in completely new ways. Rather than doing better in a given domain, these firms strive to change domains. If, for example, we compare two firms that manufacture television screens, an exploiter is likely to concentrate on improving resolution, performance, and cost of conventional TV monitors while an explorer would devote its resources to investigating flat panel displays in current and potential markets. To perform well, explorers must achieve substantial first-mover advantage. They prosper by seeing opportunities first and rapidly deploying the resources necessary to seize them. These firms are adept at developing new forms of competitive advantage and then moving on before imitators can chip away at their position.

A useful analogy that we will use repeatedly in this section is to think of the firm as a mountain climber whose goal is to climb as high as it can. Broadly speaking, the firm has a couple of options. One is to devote all its energy to climbing as high as it can up the mountain it is on now. This would involve climbing as efficiently as possible and, to the extent that the firm spends time planning and scouting, to direct that effort toward finding the best possible route up the mountain it is on. Another approach is to spend some energy and resources climbing the current mountain, but to focus on scouting other mountains in case there are higher and/or more easily climbed mountains. Clearly, the former is an exploiter and the latter an explorer.

Explorers and exploiters should, and do, have different learning behaviors. Exploiters focus on understanding more about an established terrain. They tend to display lots of incremental innovation in products and processes. The questions that guide the organization's learning originate from what it already does well and would like to do better. So, for example, a manufacturing facility might look for ways to shave a few pennies off its unit production costs, and a software development operation might focus on refining routines for documenting changes in requirements. Resources are devoted to understanding all the possible routes up the mountain and ways of covering each mountain face with less effort. These activities tend to keep the firm within the domain of the technologies, products, and customers with which it is familiar. They typically focus on serving their existing customers' needs well and on beating their current competitors.

The continual improvement methods used by Japanese automobile manufacturers in the 1980s (collectively termed the *kaizen* method) are an example of learning well suited to exploiter firms. Firms learn in the *kaizen* method by developing processes and structures that leverage the insights of the workers directly involved in the manufacturing process. Quality circles whose members are production workers are used to discover ways to improve manufacturing reliability. This kind of activity is focused on doing somewhat better what the firm is already doing. A quality circle would not be expected, for example, to propose an entirely different product or a completely novel production methodology. Rather, its focus is on improving its existing processes and products. By pointing out that an automobile headlight is sometimes damaged when the grille is put in, for example, the workers might try to see if it is possible to reverse the order of headlight and grille assembly. In this way the *kaizen* model emphasizes the power of hundreds of small incremental improvements to add up to a dramatic quality improvement or cost reduction.

Explorer firms pursue different learning paths and objectives. They go after innovations that are likely to take them outside the domains they currently occupy. They spend resources on understanding the needs of clients for whom their current products have no appeal. They encourage engineers to experiment freely with new product ideas or new ways to produce. The old Bell Labs that AT&T operated when it had a regulated monopoly on U.S. telephone service is an example of the kind of R&D facility one would expect to see at an explorer firm. Researchers there were given broad license to explore whatever avenue they thought would lead to interesting technology even when it would not be immediately useful in telephony, the company's core product line. Semiconductors were invented there in the late 1940s but were not widely used in AT&T products until the 1970s. The 3M Corporation has also been cited as a model for this kind of learning. 3M's domain has been defined broadly, and it has a history of funding product research and development for which the final application is uncertain.

One way to understand the different learning modes is to think through one of the classic models of organization learning: variation, selection, and retention (VSR). In the VSR model, successful innovations start with lots of variation. In our mountain-climbing analogy, the best way to climb higher is to collect information on many possible paths to the top of the mountain. The more paths that are explored, the more likely it is that the best path to the top will be among them. Selection occurs when the organization applies some criteria for selecting among the possible paths. In our analogy, the selection criterion is based on getting to the top while expending as few resources as are necessary to make the climb. Once the path is selected, retention occurs when the organization establishes mechanisms for ensuring that everyone stays on the selected path and moves along it expeditiously.

For example, the VSR framework can be used to help us understand how British Petroleum (BP) approached the problem of learning to drill for oil in a radically different environment than it had previously. In the 1970s, the firm had substantial experience in land-based petroleum extraction. It had gotten very good at locating and extracting oil within this familiar domain. But it now faced the problem of drilling for oil beneath the rough, cold waters of the North Sea. Dry-land extraction techniques were not well suited to this new problem. To develop new tools and techniques, the company engaged in a series of experiments designed to test a wide variety of approaches. That is, the company deliberately fostered *variation*. As the results of the experiments came in, BP had to find a way to *select* among the various approaches. Some tools or techniques clearly failed, but others were at least moderately successful and the company needed to develop routines for choosing among them. These routines required applying performance measures *and* deciding who got to make the final decisions. How much weight should be given to the engineers who ran the experiments? How much to engineers more familiar with the company's needs in other areas?

BP's solution was to allow its business unit managers to make independent judgments about which approach(es) to adopt. Although this approach allowed the firm to tailor the extraction process to the local drilling environments, it opened up the possibility that some of the knowledge it had created would be "lost." Organizational learning *(retention)* occurs when the knowledge is incorporated into the accepted ways of doing things; knowledge must be codified and disseminated through the firm if it is to contribute to the firm's capabilities. To retain innovations in an organization with decentralized decision making, BP relies on a sophisticated information technology system and a culture that support the development of personal networks among its employees.

An important difference between explorers and exploiters can be seen at the variation stage. Exploiters investigate paths on the current mountain, while explorers collect information on several mountains. If these two types search out exactly the same number of paths, the exploiter will have a better chance of finding the best way up one mountain. The explorer is less likely to find the best path up any one mountain but may find a better mountain to climb. Because the explorer looks at more mountains, the paths it investigates will have more variation. Given infinite resources applied to the problem, the explorer will do at least as well as the exploiter and will probably find a better path, that is, a path that reaches a higher altitude at less cost.[4] With limited resources, the odds that the explorer will find a better path depend on how good the exploiter's mountain is relative to all the other mountains the explorer might discover.

If the explorer organization has an advantage in the variation stage, the exploiter is better positioned for selection and retention. It will be much easier for the exploiter to figure out which of the various paths before it is the best path because it knows more about the topology of its mountain than the explorer has about the topology of the several mountains it is exploring. The exploiter faces less uncertainty. It also will find it easier to move its organization along the selected path because the organization itself is on familiar terrain. The climbers probably already have much of the equipment and training they will need. The explorer may have to invest substantial amounts in training and equipment to climb a mountain it has never encountered before.

These two business models and the forms of learning typically associated with them are supported best by different architectures, routines, and cultures. Many specific elements of ARC tend to be different in exploiters and explorers, but most of these differences are examples of just three main dimensions in which exploiters and explorers differ: the degree of interdependence among the organization's activities; the extent to which the process of change is centrally controlled; and the share of resources the firm devotes to activities outside its core domain. We discuss each of these dimensions in turn below and then describe what they mean for the ARC of exploiters and explorers.

Interdependence and Tight-Coupling

One important way in which organization designs differ is in the degree of interdependence they create among the various subunits of the firm. In Chapter 4 we introduced the terms "tightly coupled" and "loosely coupled" to describe the degree of interdependence among the subunits of an organization.

---

[4] It might be helpful to think about this process in a different way as drawing balls from urns. Each ball has a number on it, and the objective is to get a high number. The balls are divided randomly among many urns. The exploiter draws from one urn, and the explorer draws from many. Unless the exploiter's urn happens to contain the ball with the highest number, the explorer will eventually get a higher draw than the highest possible draw from the exploiters urn. The explorer's draws have more variance and are therefore more likely to result in very high (and very low) numbers.

The amount of interdependence among a firm's units is often a logical consequence of the strategy the firm is following. For example, compare the order completion process at a company like Dell that makes personal computers to order and sells directly to final customers with a company that manufactures a standardized line of computers and sells them to final customers through independent retailers. At Dell, because there are many possible configurations of computers and each is produced to order, all the elements of the process are highly interdependent. The parts must be available as soon as the order is received. Someone must be available to do the testing as soon as the computer is assembled. If an error is found, assembly must be quickly rescheduled to correct the defect. Shipping services must be immediately available when the machine is ready to go. This high degree of interdependence calls for a tightly coupled organization design: The customer order process, production scheduling, testing, and shipping departments all need to be tightly coupled if customers are to be served expeditiously. In contrast, a computer assembler producing a narrower line in much larger batches can rely on inventories to buffer any difference between order flow and operations. So, for example, production can be scheduled largely independently of product shipping because this type of computer assembler ships from finished goods inventories. It can effectively use a loosely coupled design.

Note that in this example the amount of interdependence among the firms' units is not the result of their product's characteristics because the basic technology of the product is the same for both types of computer assemblers. Instead, it is the result of how the companies have chosen to pursue competitive advantage. Dell's strategy is to sell direct, offering knowledgeable buyers lots of options without long delivery lags. Firms selling into retail channels typically sell to less technologically sophisticated buyers who have neither the knowledge nor the inclination to purchase a customized machine direct from the manufacturer. The difference in the approach to selling computers is reflected in a difference in organizational design, and tight coupling in particular. This is, indeed, another example of alignment between organization design and strategy.

As suggested in Chapter 4, many elements of ARC can contribute to more or less independence among a firm's units and hence to how tightly coupled they are. An organization structure based on functional units will usually display tighter coupling than one based on divisional units. A firm that invests resources in creating and maintaining linking mechanisms will display tighter coupling. Organizations with central routines that require tightly integrated processing—such as those that Dell has for handling customer orders—will exhibit tighter coupling, as will those whose cultures foster cooperation and good communication.

There are both advantages and disadvantages to tightly coupled designs. A tightly coupled organization is more at risk from the poor performance of a single subunit. A production process that uses just-in-time production with only minimal work-in-progress inventory, for example, can perform only as well as its least efficient unit. If one production unit falls behind temporarily, the others have no stocks of work-in-progress to fall back on and no final inventory to shield customers from the disruption. Similarly, when each unit has its own sales force, it is less affected by poor customer relations when another subunit treats a customer badly that both units share. On the other hand, the reputation for extraordinary customer service created by one subunit is equally unlikely to enhance the position of the other. Loosely coupled organizations are likely to have more redundancy than tightly coupled ones. Having multiple sales forces is a clear example of this. A tightly coupled organization is better suited to using a common resource because it has mechanisms to coordinate the sharing of resources. Similarly, it is also more likely to make use of best practice across geographies or other subunits.

The main point here is that both the tight- and loose-coupling forms can be part of consistent organizations and the degree of interdependence is a design variable for the managers of the firm. How tightly coupled the firm should be depends on its strategy and, in particular, on how it pursues competitive advantage.

Although exploiter firms can have strategies that make loose coupling of some or all of its organizational units optimal, they are usually more effective when they have a tightly coupled organization. One reason for this is that exploiter firms typically depend on efficiency for at least part of their competitive advantage and therefore want to avoid the redundancy often associated with loosely coupled organizations. Strong interdependence also allows the firm to exploit any economies of scale and replicate best practice effectively. The kind of learning pursued by an exploiter firm that is intent on deepening its competitive advantage is also well suited to a high degree of interdependence. Small, incremental changes are less likely to require substantial adjustments in other, interdependent parts of the firm. For these reasons, exploiter firms often view effective organization design as something that leads to a well-oiled machine that runs like clockwork. They deploy every possible resource to reach the well-understood objectives of the firm, each unit carrying out its own piece of the master plan. When changes are made, they are either "local" and do not affect other units, or companywide but with effects that are simple and predictable. When the adaptations required of several, interdependent units can be easily described, they also can be readily communicated through the formal and informal linking mechanisms that are in place to achieve interdependence.

Explorer firms, on the other hand, are likely to see advantages in at least some loose coupling. The extensive change necessary to create new competitive advantage is often better facilitated by a loosely coupled design. Loose coupling is beneficial because the outcome of any particular exploration is uncertain. When a unit is tightly coupled to others, it cannot explore on its own; it requires the cooperation of other units. The more that others in the organization must be induced to participate in the project, the less likely the project is to succeed. Other units may either have a different perception of the merits of the undertaking or may even stand to lose (albeit less than the organization gains) from its success. The broader the participation, the more likely that some conflict of interest will foster an internal political struggle within the organization. This can increase both the cost to the organization of pursuing the opportunity and the probability that the project will fail from a lack of wholehearted participation.

Explorers also tend to be loosely coupled so that parts of the organization can experiment without having to be concerned with how their experimentation will affect other highly interdependent parts of the firm. In tightly coupled firms, by contrast, not only must the exploratory venture obtain the cooperation of other groups within the firm, but its failure can negatively affect all of them. Even if it is eventually successful, the venture may interfere with the efficient operation of many other parts of the firm while it is being pursued. To return to the mountain-climbing metaphor, when all the climbers are roped together, no individual climber can undertake independent exploratory action without endangering the well-being of all the other climbers. It might be better to untie the exploration team from the rest of the expedition.

Organizational Slack

Organizations also vary in how much discretion they allow subunits. In some organizations, optimal performance requires that each unit fully commit its resources to reaching operational objectives. Indeed, we commonly think of "efficient" organizations as those that fully commit their resources to specified activities and seek productivity gains by wringing out waste. In this way of thinking, an efficient design is one in which resources are directed to specific, well-articulated objectives. These objectives may be established centrally or through some development process undertaken jointly by central and unit managers. However the objectives are established, all managers share them and understand that the firm's resources are to be devoted to them.

Although this is one efficient design, the resources of the firm can also be fully and efficiently utilized without common understanding of the precise way they are to be used. That is, the firm may choose to allow the unit managers complete discretion over how to deploy at least some of those resources. When resources are allocated in this way, the firm's goal is to give employees the time and resources to experiment, learn, research, think, and reflect. The rationale for this kind of investment is that it will eventually benefit the firm, though perhaps not in a way that directly affects its current performance. When funds are explicitly allocated in this way, the firms are choosing to operate with some organizational "slack." The term "slack" here does not connote waste; rather, it represents an investment in innovation and change that cannot be immediately tied to the unit's current performance.

An example of slack is a practice at 3M called "bootlegging" in which researchers are granted 15% of their work time to pursue projects of their own choosing. They are allowed this time to undertake research activities that cannot be rationalized in terms of 3M's current competitive advantage. Indeed, any useful output from these projects is likely to be outside the firm's current domain. 3M researchers have produced some of the company's important innovations (the Post-It note may be the most famous example) during their bootlegging time. Other examples of organizational slack include paying a salesperson to develop relationships with customers who have no need for the firm's existing products; providing sabbaticals to employees to pursue their own intellectual development; or sending employees to an executive education program to acquire general management skills.

Any of these "slack" activities might lead to new insights into profitable opportunities the firm might pursue, but the outcome is highly uncertain. More importantly, they are unlikely to produce the kind of incremental learning necessary for successful exploitation. For firms intent on exploiting current competitive advantage, organizational slack is unproductive. Their focus is concentrated on what they already do; experimentation that might take them far afield is not only not useful, it also wastes resources that could be put to better use within the firm's current focus. Consequently, these firms do not need organizational slack. Explorers, on the other hand, embrace organizational slack. Because non-routine or non-incremental innovations and learning often arise out of slack elements of an organization, explorers devote a relative abundance of assets to giving individuals and units the freedom to experiment and search for new ways of doing things. If the mountain climbers don't get the time to get off the current mountain, they will never discover other mountains!

Slack activities are nearly always only loosely coupled with the other activities in the organization. What a researcher does on her "own" time is, by intent, not closely connected with other activities she or others in the organization pursue as part of their contribution to the firm's current competitive advantage. While slack implies some loose coupling, the reverse claim does not hold: loose coupling does not imply organizational slack. Two units can be independent of each other, and yet each of their resources can be fully committed to specific operational objectives.

Central Direction

Organizations also vary in the extent to which their activities intended to produce change are centrally directed and coordinated. Exploiter firms are more likely to exercise centralized control of change because the cost of centralized decision making is lower for them than it is for explorer firms and the benefits are higher. The benefit of coordination is that the firm's resources can be systematically applied to move in the direction determined by central managers. A mountain-climbing team with a well-defined route will be more efficient when each member of the team knows her role and has the kinds and amount of resources she needs to fulfill it. The cost of centralization is the risk that the entire organization may be headed in the wrong direction, but this risk is relatively low for exploiter firms. They have been climbing this mountain for some time and can make well-informed choices about what kind of investments are likely to be productive.

The benefits to central coordination of change are especially high for exploiters when their operations are also tightly coupled. If changes in one part of the organization require changes in another, activities have to be coordinated. One can easily imagine a situation, for example, in which several changes made simultaneously could dramatically improve firm performance, but any of these changes made unilaterally would actually impair it. When a different unit must undertake each change, it is unlikely that all the changes will be made simultaneously or in the right sequence without some coordination. Centralized direction of resources is a particularly effective way to accomplish this.

Note that centralized control of change-oriented activities does not mean that exploiter firms maintain tight central control of all activities. Quite the contrary. Within the current domain, most of the activities pursued by exploiter firms require careful implementation of a stable strategy. As a result, these firms can delegate many routine matters. This delegation promotes efficient operation within the firm's domain and allows the senior managers to devote their attention to ensuring that any incremental changes are made in appropriate directions and are implemented in a coordinated fashion.

Central direction of change-oriented activities is much more problematic in explorer firms. For these firms, the direction of change is less certain, and benefits can accrue from allowing units to pursue independent paths. While central direction of resources does not *necessarily* imply that all units operate within the current domain, central direction is often the enemy of exploration in practice. Managers responsible for central direction inevitably have opinions about which directions might be more fruitfully pursued, and those beliefs are likely to affect which exploratory projects the firm approves. Consequently, when resources are centrally directed, the range of exploratory activities is likely to be narrower. When resource allocation for change activities is decentralized, there is less risk that the entire organization will pursue the same, necessarily risky, path.

The experience of McDonald's fast-food chain illustrates the effect of centralized direction of change. Change in the form of new product introductions and marketing innovations is essential for McDonald's to build and maintain competitive advantage. For various reasons, the McDonald's chain of fast-food outlets includes locations that are owned and operated by McDonald's employees and locations that are owned and managed by independent franchisees. Innovations introduced at the company-owned outlets are initiated and directed by the senior managers at McDonald's. At outlets owned by franchisees, the independent managers can (within the limits of their franchise agreement) experiment on their own. As our discussion of the strengths and weaknesses of centralized direction suggests, the franchised locations as a group are more innovative than the company-owned locations. Each franchisee tries things the central development group would not attempt and, since there are many independent franchisees, the range of innovations they produce is much larger than that initiated by the corporate office.

The ARC of Explorers and Exploiters

As we have argued, and as illustrated in Table 5.1, exploiters tend to rely on incremental learning and therefore typically devote more resources to the selection and retention stages of learning and less to generating variance compared to explorers. They typically have less organizational slack, are more tightly coupled, and have more centralized direction than do explorers. These differences have profound implications for the overall ARC that will be most effective for each of these two types of firms. Perhaps the most obvious difference is in the architectural structure of the organization. Because exploiters are more tightly coupled and centralized, they typically have stronger linking mechanisms and a more hierarchical decision making process.

Explorers and exploiters are also likely to have different cultures. An exploiter organization is tightly focused and task-oriented. It has low tolerance for tardiness because the high degree of interdependence means that each task dovetails with oth-

TABLE 5-1 Explorer and Exploiter Profiles

Characteristic	Exploiters	Explorers
Interdependence among units	Tightly coupled	Loosely coupled
Discretionary resources	No organizational slack	Substantial organizational slack
Direction of change-activities	Centralized	Decentralized
Learning mode	Incremental within the defined domain	Outside the defined domain
Environmental fit	Well suited to stable environments	Well suited to rapidly changing environments

ers. Hitting targets is culturally ingrained, and the firm's stories emphasize extraordinary feats of execution (the team that pulled out all the stops to get the product to the customer on time, for example). In contrast, employees at explorer organizations feel—and are—less tightly programmed. Risk-taking is encouraged, and failure is tolerated. Stories focus on the deviant behavior or extraordinary creativity that led to huge, unanticipated success. These types of firms make heroes of the employee who figured out a use (Post-its) for an apparently inadequate adhesive; or the employee who, contrary to protocol, licked his finger, discovered that the white powder on which he was working was sweet, and figured out that he had a new artificial sweetener (NutraSweet)—literally—on his hands.

Explorers and exploiters also differ in their hiring practices. Explorers need employees with a high tolerance for ambiguity and who value the process of searching for new ideas or technologies in their own right. In Silicon Valley, for example, engineers often distinguish companies and their projects in terms of a "coolness" factor. A "cool" project involves novel, cutting-edge technology, and its commercial success is often far from certain. Engineers drawn to cool projects are often less interested in the more meticulous, detailed development work that is necessary once a cool project is successfully transformed into a commercial product. Similarly, among the Web development firms clustered "South of Market" in San Francisco, the organizational cultures of the start-ups favor speed, creativity, novelty, and flair and are often (deliberately) located in old brick warehouses with exposed wooden beams rather than in more staid physical surroundings.

Exploiters have more pervasive monitoring systems and well-defined accountability because interdependencies heighten the consequences of failures-to-perform. Incentives are closely tied to specified tasks. Exploiters have numerous routines, finely honed from years of continual improvement, that ensure that all the interdependent entities are properly coordinated. In contrast, in explorer firms, incentives recognize and reward innovation. Time allocations are much less closely monitored. The firm's routines focus less on managing interdependencies among known tasks and more on identifying and developing the innovations that flow from projects. If an explorer is to harvest the fruits of its exploration, it must have routines and structures that inform management about the innovations that are produced. Their ARC must include a process both for assessing how the innovations might interact with the developments elsewhere in the firm, or might point to an entirely new direction, and for evaluating their market potential.

As should be clear by now, the distinct explorer and exploiter business models lead to firms with different competencies. Neither approach is always better. Here again the mountain-climbing analogy is useful. The exploiter will get higher up the current mountain than will the explorer because an exploiter devotes all its energy to climbing that mountain. Consequently, if the mountain being climbed is the best mountain, the exploiter will do better than the explorer. However, if a perfect mountain is just half a mile away, the exploiter will never find it, whereas the explorer may find it and then will quickly climb higher. The exploiter will outperform the explorer within a given realm of existing activity, but the explorer will do better if changing domains proves to be fruitful.

Managers who are introduced to the explorer–exploiter distinction can readily tell which label better describes their firm (or at least their part of the firm). That is the strength of the explorer–exploiter concept. By understanding the firm's explorer and exploiter competencies and organizational underpinnings, the manager is better able to predict how the firm will perform at maintaining and changing its competitive advantage over time. He will recognize the competencies the firm's organization gives to its pursuit of competitive advantage. He will also understand the limitations those competencies create for the realm of activities in which the firm is weak.

For example, managers in exploiter firms often lament that it is always the firm's competitors that first seize new opportunities that (with hindsight) their own firm ought to have captured. They will even sometimes complain that they had the same idea themselves but couldn't get the attention of, or resources from, more senior mangers to develop it. It is little consolation to them to know that the firm missed the opportunity not because it is badly managed, but because *it is well managed to operate within its current domain*. By focusing well on its current domain, a well-managed exploiter inevitably misses opportunities. Conversely, managers in explorer organizations will lament that other firms reap the benefits of their innovations while they watch their original dominant market share dwindle. Again the fact that this fate is part of the firm's destiny (and strength) as an explorer does not necessarily ease their pain.

Knowing why the firm is behaving as it is may not make the firm's deficiencies easier to swallow, but it is an important first step in diagnosis and change. A manager who knows, for example, that the firm's success at exploitation makes it weak in exploration is more likely to think about when exploitation alone is likely to fail the firm than a manager who is unaware of the problem. He may be more attuned to changes in the environment that portend a weakened competitive position because competitors have opened new domains than a manager who has no idea that new domains are possible. He also may devote resources to some exploration, while maintaining the focus on the firm's current domain. To do this effectively, he will need to find some way to combine exploration and exploitation within the same firm. In the next section, we turn to the problems he is likely to encounter in this effort.

5.4 COMBINING EXPLORATION AND EXPLOITATION

If both exploration and exploitation have advantages, it is natural to think about doing both. Why can't a firm have the best of both worlds and be the consummate explorer and the most efficient exploiter? The reason is that it is hard to be good at both; the optimal organizational designs consistent with each approach are so different. One is loosely coupled, the other tightly coupled. One embraces organizational slack, the other deploys all its resources to explicit ends. As already discussed, the organizational implications go beyond these differences to include many other elements of ARC. The very organizational design elements that make firms good at exploiting are likely to inhibit exploring, and vice versa. Consequently, no firm can be a world-class exploiter and explorer at the same time.

However, pure explorer and pure exploiter firms are unlikely to survive over the long haul. Firms may, for example, be successful at exploiting a current competitive advantage within a stable environment for many years. Inevitably, however, the environment will change to make that competitive advantage no longer advantageous. Other firms catch up, or the landscape changes. Anticipating this eventuality, and perhaps wanting to be in the forefront of any change that promises new opportunities, most exploiter firms devote some resources to exploratory activities. Similarly, a pure explorer is unlikely to be successful. Once an explorer discovers something new, it generally will want to become pretty good at it. It is nice to come up with the Post-It note, but once you have it, you want to make the most of it—to exploit it, in fact. If the firm is not good at exploiting its innovation, imitators will eventually overtake it.

There are only two ways to survive, even in the medium term, as a pure explorer. One way is if the innovations the firm creates are protected by some barrier to imitation of the kind discussed in Chapter 3 that prevent more efficient exploiters from taking over the market. If the firm continues to explore, however, most of the new opportunities it uncovers will probably not enjoy these kinds of barriers. Generally, sustainable competitive advantage requires some investment by the firm, the kind of investment in which exploiter firms are proficient. The other path along which a pure explorer might find some success is to enjoy its first-mover advantage for as long as it can and then move on to the next venture. For example, 3M recently divested a division that manufactured floppy disks, blank VHS tapes, and similar products because this division performed poorly under 3M's management. As these markets became commodity markets with many competitors, 3M's first-mover advantage deteriorated, and the burden of inefficient operations became unsupportable. It is therefore not coincidental that pure explorer firms are rare. Those who have explored successfully but have failed at exploiting the fruits of their exploration have long since disappeared. Either they have failed, or, as with many biotechnology firms, they have been acquired by successful established firms with the capabilities necessary for exploitation.

Since it is difficult for a firm to survive as either a pure explorer or a pure exploiter, the issue, then, is how a firm can combine elements of both. For a variety of reasons, this is perhaps even more difficult than excelling at either pure form. However, while challenging, it is the job of senior management to develop and nurture an ARC that enables the firm to chart a course between the extremes. Generally, this requires navigating gray areas in which both exploration and exploitation are prized.

To accomplish this, a firm must build a culture that fits both exploration and exploitation. It is difficult, however, for the same firm to make heroes of both renegade explorers and consummate exploiters. To the employees who are devoted to exploitation, the explorers look like reckless adventurers who depend on luck and live off the hard work of the exploiters in the firm. The exploiters also know that if these adventurers succeed, they might endanger the careers of the exploiters. The explorers, on the other hand, have little sympathy for the processes on which exploiters depend. They tend to view exploiters as unduly bound to old ways of seeing the world and blind to the opportunities that lie all around. Although it might be clear what culture to prescribe for explorers or exploiters, it is more difficult for a culture to support a hybrid organization because its norms and values must tolerate more ambiguity. Managing a hybrid organization requires a culture that allows diversity.

The architecture of the firm also must support both exploratory and exploitative activity. Within most firms, there are many units that are basically exploiters in their approach. Though focused on exploitation, occasionally these units will nonetheless spawn new opportunities that could open up new domains for the firm. Often it is middle managers who must recognize and bring forward the new opportunities that arise out of the work of their units. The advantage of giving this responsibility to these managers is that they are the managers most familiar with what their units have produced; other managers may have no way to recognize the new development. The problem is that the same managers who are charged with exploitation are also responsible for nurturing exploration. If they are to do both, the rewards for these activities must be carefully balanced. If the rewards to exploration are too high, achieving consistently superior exploitation will be difficult because managers will focus on exploration. On the other hand, if all of the focus is on performing well at exploitation, managers will have no incentive to champion good ideas that might take the firm into new domains.

Although making managers responsible for both exploitation and exploration is the most common approach, some firms separate responsibility for these functions. They have people in some units focused on exploitation, while others, usually in senior management, focus on exploration. A related approach is to concentrate the responsibility for exploration within one functional unit. In many firms, the business development function has responsibility for overseeing and nurturing the firm's exploration. The advantage of separating exploratory and exploitative behavior is that some units can focus on exploiting within the firm's current domain without being distracted by exploration, while others are responsible for scouting out new possible domains without having to sustain the firm's current competitive advantage.

Even when responsibility is separated in this way, neither senior management nor the business development group conducts much of the actual exploration themselves. Instead, their responsibility is to scan the firm for promising new developments and assess the opportunities they represent. Scanning the firm is productive because even units that are pure exploiters in their intent will learn serendipitously outside their current domain. This especially occurs in technology-driven organizations in which R&D directed at one problem often unexpectedly yields fruitful results for another. However, in pure exploiter organizations, such opportunities will tend to be lost because everyone is so focused on exploitation that they pay little attention to learning that might take them outside the current domain. An active and perceptive business development group or group of senior managers can try to capture and mold those opportunities.

Some firms have gone even further and have attempted to divide their exploration and exploitation activities between different divisions. One firm renowned for following the divisional solution to the problem is the Xerox Corporation with its Palo Alto Research Center (PARC). Although Xerox was highly focused on the photocopier market, Xerox PARC was given resources to indulge in a wide variety of research activities not explicitly related to photocopiers. Moreover, the researchers were also given the freedom to pursue research of their own interests without any master plan of where the research would take the company. This investment in organizational slack was extraordinarily productive. Many of the innovations that characterized the PC revolution originated at Xerox PARC, including the mouse and the graphical user interface that inspired the Apple Macintosh and, indirectly, Microsoft's Windows-based operating system. Xerox PARC also produced the ethernet, one of the key initial systems from which the current Internet developed. It seems unlikely that Xerox Parc would have achieved this rich array of innovation if its engineers had been asked to focus on the demands of Xerox's competitive advantage in photocopying.

At first blush, it seems that Xerox was able to be both a good exploiter in photocopying and a good explorer in other domains. However, it is not enough for a firm that is good at exploitation in its current domain simply to explore in others. It must also be able to reap the benefits of that exploration. Although Xerox PARC produced many incredibly valuable innovations, Xerox Corporation rarely captured the value of these innovations. Instead, it let firms like Apple exploit the innovations. Xerox's inability to capture value from these innovations was not a result of poor management. Rather, it arose precisely because Xerox was so well managed and well designed to exploit the domain of copiers. The research outputs at Xerox PARC were not useful for Xerox's current competitive advantage, and Xerox had no structures or processes in place to capture value from activities that were far afield from its current domain. Indeed, only because Xerox was extremely successful in the copier business did it have the luxury of supporting unrelated exploratory activity that produced little benefit for the firm.

The point here is twofold. First, firms need both to exploit and explore if they are to perform well over the long run. Second, it is not enough for a firm that is good at exploiting its current advantage also to be good at discovering potentially profitable new domains. The firm must also find a way to exploit these opportunities by integrating them into the firm's strategy. Xerox had a well-defined strategy in copiers, but it had no way to alter or extend its strategy to exploit the opportunities Xerox PARC developed. In the language of the variation-selection-retention model introduced earlier, Xerox PARC was superb at generating variation, but Xerox had no mechanisms to select among the many promising developments and no way to exploit (retain) them. The challenge managers face is both to explore and to exploit within the same firm *and* to make the strategic changes necessary to reap the benefits from exploration.

5.5 COSTS OF ORGANIZATIONAL CHANGE

Before moving on we want to note that undertaking organizational change that might help deepen or change a firm's competitive advantage has costs as well as benefits. The costs can be of two types. First, the uncertainty employees are exposed to when the organization is changed tends to lead to lower productivity and increased turnover during the transition. No matter how well designed the process of change might be, it takes time for people to understand and come to terms with how new incentives will be implemented, how new routines will be specified, and how new values will be enacted. Second, the overall organization will probably go through a period in which the design is worse than it was before the change was undertaken. It is difficult—if not impossible—to alter several elements of an organization at once if only because some aspects of the organization are easier to change than others. To return to the transportation metaphor, the new road system may be much better than the old, but while the roads are torn up to build the new system, traffic conditions deteriorate. All organization change takes time, and periods of transition when things do not work well are inevitable. Some changes take longer than others. Architectural elements typically can be changed more quickly than routines and culture. This also means that the disruption to operations is more intense when the firm needs to change several elements because the firm must then endure a period when some of the new design is in place, but the other elements have not yet adjusted.

Although we have argued that a firm must be organized to accommodate both continual exploitation and exploration, we do not mean that a company should be continuously changing its organization design. While organization change is sometimes necessary, it also has both coordination and incentive effects that should not be underestimated. At least in the short term, change will tend to disrupt coordination. Because change requires that individuals figure out new ways to address old tasks and solve new ones, coordination will be more difficult in moving to a new design. Moreover, if change within an organization continues over an extended period, it is likely to weaken incentives by eroding employees' beliefs that behaviors and outcomes valued today will be valued tomorrow. If an employee cannot be confident about what behavior or activities will be rewarded in the future, she is likely to avoid expending effort that has only a long-term payoff. If a company frequently changes its structure, for example, employees become less willing to take the time and energy to form good working relationships because they know that the relationships will probably not last long.

The challenge is not to change the organization design continually, but to create a design that will accommodate change in the firm's activities. Sometimes, however, the strategic change the firm needs to make is so substantive that a major change in organizational design is required and justified. The issue of strategic change is a major subject of Chapters 11 and 15. There are also some unique organizational issues that confront global organizations, and we examine those in Chapter 13.

5.6 SUMMARY

In this chapter we argued that the firm's organization must not only be internally consistent it must also be aligned with its strategy. We also emphasized that the firm's competitive advantage is likely to change over time and that how the firm learns and, therefore, its capacity to seek new competitive advantage is governed by its approach to exploitation and exploration.

We have also seen that for a firm to engage in effective strategic change, it is not enough to explore new possible forms of competitive advantage. It must also capture new competitive advantages in coherent and logical strategies and put an organization and resources in place that can capitalize on the opportunities that the exploration uncovers. As Jim March noted in introducing the explorer and exploiter terminology, "maintaining an appropriate balance between exploration and exploitation is a primary factor in ... survival and prosperity."[5] We emphasized that the costs of organizational change must be factored in when attempting to change the balance.

We turn our attention now from the firm's internal context to its external context. Just as we have introduced a framework for analyzing the firm's internal context, we introduce a framework for understanding its external context. The next few chapters, then, will introduce the tools managers need to assess the challenges and opportunities in their firms' external context.

---

[5] James March, *ibid*, 71.

INDEX

A
Abrahams, Jeffrey, 24n
Acquisitions, 368, 399
Actions, in oligopoly, 188, 189–197
Advance sign-ups, 325
Aguilar, Francis J., 9n, 30n
Airbus, 44, 141–142, 189
Alcoa, 237
Amazon.com, 37–38, 217
Amdahl Corporation, 147
American Airlines, 207, 208, 237, 319n
American National Standards Institute (ANSI), 326
American Tobacco, 212
America Online (AOL), 40, 319
Anderson, Philip, 296n
Antitrust, 211–213
   collusion in, 211–213
   entry barriers and, 236–237
   interfirm agreements and, 202–203, 213
   price discrimination and, 268–269
   price predation in, 211
Apple Computer, 11, 46, 101, 166, 295, 311, 315, 317, 318
Applied Materials, mission statement of, 26n
ARC analysis, 75–90
   architecture in, 75, 76–86, 89–90
   competitive advantage and, 95–103, 111–113
   coordination problem and, 87–90, 91
   culture in, 76, 88–90
   of multibusiness company, 371–377
   organization design and, 75–90, 371–377
   routines in, 76, 86–88, 89–90
   strategic alignment and, 97–100
Architecture
   compensation and rewards, 82–86
   defined, 75
   firm performance and, 371–373
   structure, 76–82, 343–345
Armco, 122–123
Asea Brown Boveri (ABB), 12, 83
Asset analysis, 35–36
Asymmetric information, in games. *See* Game theory
AT&T, 50–51, 105, 131, 150
Autonomous strategy process, 381, 395–397

B
Bain, Joe S., 124n
Bandwagon effect, 322, 323
Bargaining power, 251–254
Barney, Jay B., 53, 53n
Baron, David P., 120n
Baron, James, 73n
Bartlett, Christopher A., 348n
Benchmarking
   compensation and, 84
   with market transactions, 257
   of transfer prices, 85
Benetton, 155–157, 293, 332
Benkard, C. Lanier, 224n
Bennis, Warren, 27, 27n
Bertrand equilibrium. *See* Game theory
Bethlehem Steel, 122–123, 208
Bias, compensation and, 84
BIC Company, 56–57, 229–230
Blockbuster Entertainment Group, mission statement of, 24

Boeing Corporation, 44, 52, 141–142, 153–154, 189, 337
Bootlegging, 109–110
Borders, Inc., 31–32, 34, 36, 37–38, 391–392
Boston Consulting Group, 399, 400
Bower, Joseph L., 297n
Branding, 44, 85–86
Bresnahan, Timothy, 163n, 167n, 231, 232
British Petroleum (BP), 105–106, 343
Brock, Gerald, 206n
Brock, James, 272n
Brown, Shona L., 401n
Bundling, and price discrimination, 267
Burgelman, Robert A., 15, 15n, 299, 394n
Business development function, 115
Business strategy, 2–10, 19–38
   corporate strategy versus, 351–352
   describing, 19–23
   dynamics of, 6–8
   goals of, 3–4
   mission statement and, 24–27
   nature of, 12–13
   strategy process and, 33–38, 383–390
   strategy statement, 28–32
Buyer power
   bargaining with powerful suppliers, 251–254
   change and, 276
   in Structure-Conduct-Performance (SCP) paradigm, 126–127
   value capture and, 247–254
   in value chain analysis, 143, 244
   vertical power, 140–142
Buyer preferences, 305–306

C

Canon, 166, 303, 333–334
Capability advantage, 49–55
   kinds of capabilities, 46–48
   positional advantage versus, 41–43
   relationship to positional advantage, 51–55
   as sustainable competitive advantage, 49–50
Capacity, in oligopoly, 190–197
Carroll, Glenn R., 282n, 286
Causal ambiguity, 49
Caves, Richard, 139n
Centralized structure, 110–111, 344–345
Chandler, Alfred, 78–79
Change, strategic, 36–38, 271–304
   barriers to, 294–301
   and competitive advantage, 274–277
   costs of, 117
   in evolution of automobile industry, 272–274
   in evolution of industry organization, 287–294
   in evolution of strategy, 389–390, 393–397
   and industry life cycle, 277–287
   managing, 294–304
Characteristics maps, 157–161
Charles Schwab, 394
Cheap talk, 202
Christensen, Clayton M., 297n, 298
Chrysler, 207, 262, 273, 339
Ciba-Geigy, 331
Cisco Systems, 51, 153
Clark, Kim B., 297, 297n
Clayton Act, 237
Coca-Cola Company, 1, 12, 172, 209, 210, 226
Collectivism-individualism, 338–339
Collis, David J., 360n
Collusion, 211–213
Commitment problem, 377, 416. See also Game theory
Compaq Computer, 4–6, 7
Compatibility benefits
   for demand-side increasing returns, 306–308, 317–318
   system compatibility, 317–318

Compensation, 82–86
Competency trap, 296–298
Competition
   change and, 275–276
   in concentrated markets. *See* Dominant firm structure; Oligopoly
   and market share, 168–169
   in markets with demand-side increasing returns, 311–317
      competitive strategies for building DSIR, 315–317
      installed base and tipping, 311–315
   and product differentiation, 165–169
   product positioning and, 170–172
   spectrum of, 150–154. *See also* Spectrum of competition
   strategy of, 386–387
   in Structure-Conduct-Performance (SCP) paradigm, 126–127
   in value chain analysis, 136–138, 139–140, 142
Competitive advantage, 39–63, 93–118
   ARC analysis and, 95–103, 111–113
   and business strategy, 21–22
   capability, 41–43, 46–48, 49–55, 66
   central direction and, 110–111
   change and, 274–277
   cost-quality frontier and, 59–62
   culture and, 89
   exploiters and, 94, 103–106, 108, 109–116
   explorers and, 94, 103–106, 108–110, 111–116
   interdependence and tight-coupling, 106–109
   organizational slack and, 109–110
   organization design and, 65–67, 93–118
   positional, 41–46, 50–55, 66
   and resource-based view of the firm, 53–55
   strategic alignment for, 95–101
   strategic spillovers and, 361–366
   in strategy process, 382
   sustainable, 48–51
   value and, 39–40
Complements
   industry definitions of, 146–147
   nature of, 132
   price discrimination and, 266–267
   switching costs and, 228
Computer Associates, 313
Concentrated markets, 185–214
   antitrust and, 211–213, 236–237, 268–269
   defined, 185
   See also Dominant firm structure; Oligopoly
Conglomerate form, 360–361
Conner Peripherals, 298
Conscious parallelism doctrine, 212
Consistency, organizational, 99–100
Consumer loyalty, incumbency advantage from, 226
Consumer preferences
   characteristics maps and, 157–161
   and product differentiation, 157–162
Contingency planning, 302
Continual improvement methods, 104
Contracts
   as entry barriers, 235
   explicit, 263
   relational, 256–257
Control Data Corporation (CDC), 316
Coordination problem, 71–73, 74–75
   ARC analysis and, 89–90, 91
   corporate culture and, 88–89
   in incentives and rewards, 82–86
   organizational structure and, 79–82
   routinization and, 87, 374
   strategic alignment and, 96–97
   value creation and, 257–260
Corn Flakes, 160, 163, 165, 179, 180, 182
Corporate direction, 377–378
Corporate strategy, 12–13
   business strategy versus, 351–352
   framework for, 356–357

Corporate strategy *(continued)*
  strategic spillovers, 354–356, 358, 361–366
  strategy processes, 397–403
    role of general managers in, 402–403
    for strategically independent businesses, 398–401
    for strategically interdependent businesses, 401–402
  See also Multibusiness company
Cost-quality frontier, 55–62
  framework for, 58–59
  to illustrate competitive advantage, 59–62
  product quality and cost, 56–58
Cournot equilibrium. *See* Game theory
Creative destruction, 294
Creative process, 382
Credibility, in competition. *See* Game theory
Cross-functional teams, at Southwest Airlines, 68–69, 70–71, 97–99
Crown Cork & Seal, 332
Culture
  coordination problem and, 88–89
  defined, 76
  and exploitation/exploration, 115. *See also* Exploiters; Explorers
  incentive problem and, 89
  of Southwest Airlines, 69
Cumulative investment, as entry barrier, 222–226
Customer relationship, and positional advantage, 44
Customized components, 258–259

D

Daimler-Benz, 85, 339
Deadweight loss (DWL), 175
Dean Witter, 365–366
Decline stage, 286–287
De facto standards, 45, 326–327
De jure standards, 327
Dell Computer, 4–6, 12, 107, 254, 290
Demand-side increasing returns (DSIR), 228, 305–328, 386
  competition in markets with, 311–317
    competitive strategies for building, 315–317
    installed base and tipping, 311–315
  nature of, 305–306
  sources of, 306–310
    compatibility benefits, 306–308, 317–318
    network benefits, 308–310
  standards-setting processes, 326–328
  systems of components, 317–321
    leveraging market position, 318–321
    system compatibility, 317–318
  technology adoption, 321–326
    managing, 323–326
    nature of, 321–323
Digital Equipment Corporation (DEC), 5
Direct Satellite Broadcasting (DSB), 51
Disney Corporation, 24, 50, 354–357, 358, 376
Distinctive competence, 47–48
Distribution channels, and positional advantage, 45
Diversification, 359–361, 366, 368–369, 376
Divestiture strategy, 368*n*, 399
Divisional organization, 77, 78–79, 81, 82–86
Dominant firm structure
  defined, 186
  market structure and firm behavior, 154
  nature of, 151, 152–153, 209
  persistence of, 209–210
Dominion Engineering, 45
Double marginalization, 250–251
DSIR. *See* Demand-side increasing returns (DSIR)
DuPont, 78–79, 295

Durable productive assets, switching costs of, 227

E
Early adopters, 323
Eastman Kodak, 7, 186, 296–297
eBay, 230, 313, 314
Economies of scale, 23
    global efficiency and, 340–342
    incumbency advantage and, 217–222
    minimum efficient scale (MES), 220–222, 332–333
    in multibusiness company, 364
Economies of scope
    incumbency advantage from, 229–231
    in multibusiness company, 364
EDS, 153, 209, 367
Eisenhardt, Kathleen M., 401n
Eli Lilly, 332–333, 363
Elzinga, Kenneth K., 284, 285
Emergence stage, 278–282
EMI, 39–40, 280, 365
Entry barriers
    antitrust and, 236–237
    change and, 276
    cumulative investment, 222–226
    economies of scale, 217–222
    examples of, 138–140
    learning economies, 223–225
    nature of, 138, 216
    signaling, 235–236
    in Structure-Conduct-Performance (SCP) paradigm, 126–127
    theory of, 231–232
    in value chain analysis, 138–140, 142
    vertical foreclosure, 235
    See also Incumbency advantage
Essential facility, 211
European Union (EU), 213, 335
Evolutionary economics, 14, 15
Exit costs, 286–287
Experience goods, incumbency advantage from, 226–227
Explicit contracts, 263
Exploiters
    accountabilities in, 112–113
    ARC analysis of, 111–113
    centralized control of, 110–111
    exploration by, 114–116
    intentional process and, 397
    nature of, 94, 103–106
    organizational slack and, 109, 110
    tight coupling of, 108
Explorers
    ARC analysis of, 111–113
    autonomous processes and, 397
    decentralization of, 111
    exploitation by, 114–116
    globalization and, 333–334, 342–344
    hiring practices of, 112
    loose coupling of, 108–109
    nature of, 94, 103–106
    organizational slack and, 109, 110
Extensive form games. *See* Game theory
External environment, 43, 65
    business strategy evaluation in, 386–387
    defined, 2–3

F
FCB-Publicis, 80
Federation structure, 344–345
Financial capital, 367–369
Fine, Charles H., 278n, 291
Fiorina, Carly, as CEO of HP, 356
Firm
    concept of, 12–13
    performance of, 371–373
Firm behavior, nature of, 153–154
First-mover advantage, 6, 171, 198
Five Forces, 124–127
Fixed costs, 217–219
Flat organization, 79
Ford Motor Company, 146–147, 160–161, 171, 185, 207, 262, 274, 342–343, 361
Freeman, John, 14n

Fuji-Xerox, 302–304, 326
Functional organization, 77–78

G

Game theory, 405–426
   credibility, commitment, and flexibility, 416–421
   effect of repetition, 414–416
   Nash equilibrium and duopoly, 410–414
   prisoners' dilemma, 406–410
   strategic behavior and asymmetric information, 422–425
Gap, The, 155–157, 172, 185
Gatekeepers, and positional advantage, 45
Gates, Bill, 306, 315
General Electric (GE), 9–10, 40, 78–79, 145, 368, 372, 375, 378, 399, 400
General manager
   and goals of strategic management, 3–4
   impact of, 14–16
   nature of, 13
   role in corporate strategy process, 13, 15–16, 402–403
General Motors (GM), 2, 6–7, 160–161, 171, 206–207, 254–257, 273–274, 299–301, 345, 367
Geographic incumbency, and positional advantage, 45
Georgia-Pacific, 46, 47
Ghemawat, Pankaj, 2n, 48n
Ghoshal, Sumantra, 348n
Giveaways, 315–316
Global efficiency, 340–342
Globalization, 7, 329–349
   implications for managers, 330–332
   of industries and economies, 334–335
   organization structure in, 344–349
   and product differentiation, 167
   strategic challenges, 335–349
      global efficiency, 340–342
      learning, 333–334, 342–344
      local responsiveness, 336–340
      organizing for, 344–349
      strategic gains from, 332–334
Goals
   and business strategy, 20–21
   of strategic management, 3–4
Government protection and support, and positional advantage, 44–45
Grant, Robert M., 48, 48n
Grove, Andrew S., 288, 288n
Growth stage, 283–284

H

Hall, Bronwyn, 122, 123
Hamel, Gary, 52, 52n
Hamermesh, Richard, 9n
Hannan, Michael T., 14n, 282n, 286
Harrod's, 93
Hasselblad, 250
Henderson, Rebecca M., 297, 297n
Hewlett-Packard, 12, 79, 88, 297, 299–301, 351, 356
Hidden action, 74. *See also* Game theory
Hidden information, 74. *See also* Game theory
Hirschman-Herfindahl Index (HHI), 137
Hofstede, Geert H., 338
Honda, 171, 337, 394
Horizontal communication, 343–344
Horizontal differentiation, 161
Horizontal linkages, in organizational structure, 80–82, 343–344
Horizontal organization, of industry, 287–292
Human capital, 369–371
Hurwicz, 139n

I

IBM, 50–51, 146, 147, 152–153, 166, 210, 266–267, 280, 288, 295, 316, 319, 324, 326

Incentive problem, 73–75
　ARC analysis and, 89–90, 91
　coordination problem and, 82–86
　culture and, 89
　routines and, 87–88
　strategic alignment and, 96–97
　value creation and, 260–263
Incumbency advantage, 138–140
　from consumer loyalty, 226
　from cumulative investment, 222–226
　from demand-side increasing returns, 228
　nature of, 215–216
　through packing product space, 232–235
　scale advantages, 217–222
　scope economies and, 229–231
　strategic creation of, 232–237
　from sunk costs, 229
　from switching costs, 227–228
　and uncertain product quality, 226–227
　See also Entry barriers
Individualism-collectivism, 338–339
Industry analysis, 119–147
　competition in, 136–138, 139–140, 142
　entry barriers in, 138–140
　example of, 133–136, 142–144
　framework, 127–144
　industry definition in, 144–147
　industry map in, 386–387
　organizing, 123–127
　performance effects of industry characteristics, 120–123
　Structure-Conduct-Performance (SCP) paradigm, 124–127
　value capture in, 136
　value creation in, 129–136
　vertical power in, 140–142
Industry definition, 144–147
Industry life cycle, 277–287
　decline, 286–287
　emergence, 278–282
　growth, 283–284
　maturity, 284–286
Industry structure, 287–294
　horizontal versus vertical, 287–292
　organizational implications of, 292–294
Influence, 325, 374–375
Information
　diversification and, 369, 376
　in oligopoly, 188, 200–202
　routines for, 373–374
　signaling and, 200–202
　types of, 200
Innovation
　as entry barrier, 225–226
　recognizing value of, 343–344
Installed base, 45, 311–315
Intel, 153, 166, 288, 305, 311, 318
Intellectual property rights, 325–326
Intentional strategy process, 381, 395–397
Interdependence
　nature of, 81–82
　and tight-coupling, 106–109
Interfirm agreements, 202–203, 213
Internal context, 43, 65
　business strategy evaluation in, 385–386
　defined, 2–3
Internationalization. *See* Globalization
Intervention, 375–377
Investment, as entry barrier, 222–226

J
Johnson & Johnson, 85, 375, 376–377

K
Kaizen method, 104
Keller, Greg, 160*n*
Kellogg's, 160, 165, 166, 237
Kirin, 336–337
Kmart, 93
Kodak, 7, 186, 296–297
Kreps, David M. 73*n*

L

Lamont, Owen, 81*n*
Lang, Larry H. P., 359*n*
Larson, Andrea, 262*n*
Lazear, 73*n*
Learning economies, 223–225
Leasing, 326
Liaison role, 80
Liggett & Meyers, 212
Limit pricing, 236
Line managers, in strategy process, 396
Litman, Barry, 329*n*
LL Bean, 46
Local adaptation, 345
Local responsiveness, 336–340
Location, switching costs of, 228
Locational advantage, 346–348, 349
Lockheed, 224
Logic
  and business strategy, 22–23
  logical incrementalism, 15
Loosely coupled organizations, 82, 106–109
Lotus, 325–326
Loyalty programs, switching costs of, 228

M

Management levels
  line managers, 396
  middle management, 396
  senior management, 83, 115, 382–383, 396
March, James, 94*n*, 104, 118, 118*n*, 296–297
Market position, leveraging, 318–321
Market segmentation, niche markets and, 163–165
Market share, and competition, 168–169
Market structure, nature of, 153–154
Market value to asset value, 121–123
Marks & Spencer, 44, 337
Mason, Edward S., 124*n*
Matsushita, 344–345
Maturity stage, 284–286
McDonald's, 58, 111
McGahan, Anita M., 122*n*, 160*n*
McKinsey and Co., 363–364, 399, 400
Merck, 46, 295, 364
Metcalfe's law, 308*n*
Microsoft, 128–129, 153, 166, 306, 314, 315, 318–319, 320–321, 324, 362, 389–390
Middle managers, in strategy process, 396
Miller, 159, 161
Minimum efficient scale (MES), 220–222, 332–333
Mintzberg, Henry, 13, 13*n*
Mission statement, 24–27
  example of, 25–26
  in strategic plans, 391
Mobility barriers, 171–172, 210
Monopoly
  market structure and firm behavior, 154
  nature of, 150–152, 173–176
  value capture in, 247–249
Mont Blanc, 56–57
Monteverde, Kirk, 274*n*
Montgomery, Cynthia A., 53, 53*n*, 360*n*
Morgan Stanley Dean Witter, 366
Motorola, 331
Multibusiness company, 351–379
  adding value, 358–361
  corporate direction, 377–378
  organization design, 371–377
  performance of diversified firms, 359–361
  resource allocation, 356–357, 367–371
  strategic spillovers, 354–356, 358, 361–366
  strategy process of, 397–403
  See also Corporate strategy
Murdoch, Rupert, 236

N

Nanus, Burt, 27, 27n
Nash equilibrium, 410–414
National culture
  individualism-collectivism, 338–339
  power distance, 338, 339
Natural monopoly, 51
Nelson, Richard, 15, 15n
Netscape, 315, 389–390
Network effects, 80, 228, 308–310
Nevo, Aviv, 158n
New United Motor Manufacturing Inc. (NUMMI), 256–257, 260
Niche markets
  and demand-side increasing returns, 315, 316–317
  example of, 155–157
  market segments in, 163–165
  market structure and firm behavior, 154
  nature of, 151, 152, 154–155, 178–183
  product differentiation and, 154–157
Nike, 44, 85, 335, 361
Noise, compensation and, 84
Nordstrom, 44
Norm of reciprocity, 88
North American Free Trade Agreement (NAFTA), 335
Northern Telecom, 185
Novo-Nordisk, 81, 332–333
Nucor, 122–123
NutraSweet, 112, 150, 383

O

Objectives
  performance, 10–12
  statement of, 382
Ohmae, Kenichi, 346
Oligopoly, 186–209
  actions in, 188, 189–197
  defined, 186
  information in, 188, 200–202
  market structure and firm behavior, 154
  nature of, 151, 153, 186–187
  players in, 187, 199–200
  repetition in, 188, 202–208
  timing in, 188, 197–199
OPEC cartel, 247
Open standard, 325
Opportunity analysis, 35–36
Opportunity cost of resources, 129–130
Option value, 229
O'Reilly, Charles, 68n
Organizational ecology, 14
Organizational slack, 109–110
Organizational structure, 6–7, 76–82
  compensation and, 82–86
  coordination and, 79–82
  divisional organization, 77, 78–79, 81, 82–86
  federated versus centralized, 344–345
  flat organization, 79
  functional organization, 77–78
  in globalization, 344–349
  horizontal linkages in, 80–82, 343–344
  structure of technology and, 297
  tall organization, 79
Organizational uncertainty, 280–281
Organization design, 65–92
  ARC analysis and, 75–90, 371–377
  architecture in, 75, 76–86, 89–90
  and competitive advantage, 65–67, 93–118
  coordination problem, 71–73, 74–75, 80–86, 89–90
  culture in, 76, 88–90
  incentive problem, 73–75, 82–86, 89–90
  organizational consistency and, 99–100
  routines in, 76, 86–88, 89–90
  at Southwest Airlines, 67–71
  strategic alignment and, 95
  and strategy process, 383

Organization learning, 105–106
  globalization and, 333–334, 342–344
  learning economies, 223–225

P

Pacific Bell, 144–145
Packing the product space, 232–235
Pascale, Richard T., 394n
Patagonia, 11
Penetration pricing, 315–316
Penrose, Edith T., 53, 53n
PepsiCo, 85, 209, 210, 226, 254
Perceptual maps, 157–161
Perfect competition, nature of, 151, 152, 176–178
Performance effects
  examples of, 120–121
  and market value to asset value, 121–123
  nature of, 120
Performance objectives, 10–12
Periphery, 298–299
Pfeffer, Jeffrey, 68n
Philips, 334, 344
Pirating, 325–326
Players, in oligopoly, 187, 199–200
Porter, Michael E., 53, 60, 60n, 122n, 124–127, 136, 346–348, 359, 359n
Positional advantage, 41–46, 50–55, 66
  capability advantage versus, 41–43
  examples of, 44–46
  forms of, 43–44
  general characteristics of, 45–46
  relationship to capability advantage, 51–55
  as sustainable competitive advantage, 50–51
Positive feedback, from installed based, 312–315
Potential industry earnings (PIE), 129–144
  change and, 274–276
  competition and, 136–138, 142
  determinants of, 130–133
  dividing, 136–144
  entry barriers and, 138–140, 142
  example of, 133–136
  incumbency advantage and, 216
  monopoly and, 173–176
  niche markets and, 178–183
  perfect competition and, 176–178
  in value creation and value capture, 239–242
  vertical power and, 140–142
Power distance, 338, 339
Prahalad, C. K., 52, 52n
Predatory pricing, 211, 236–237, 315–316
Price commitments, 326
Price discrimination, 175, 264–269
  antitrust restrictions on, 268–269
  bundling and, 267
  perfect, 265
  re-sale prevention and, 268
  time and, 267
  willingness to pay and, 265–267
Price fixing, 211–213
Procter & Gamble, 45–46, 85, 242, 345, 364, 366
Product differentiation, 6, 137–138
  and competition, 165–169
  consumer preferences and, 157–162
  example of, 155–157
  horizontal, 161
  niche markets and, 154–157
  vertical, 161–162
Productivity, wages and, 341–342
Product positioning, 170–172
Profitability
  compensation and, 82–86
  performance effects of industry characteristics and, 120–123
Profit maximization, 11–12, 20–21, 82
Promotional advantage, as entry barrier, 226
Public sector, 120, 327, 333

Q

Quality
  in cost-quality frontier, 55–62
  incumbency advantage and, 226–227
Quality circles, 104
Quantum, 298
Quigley, Joseph, 28n
Quinn, James Brian, 15, 15n

R

Rank Organization, 303
Ravenscraft, David J., 360n
Real options. *See* Game theory
Regional organization, 346
Reiss, Peter, 231, 232
Relational contracts, 256–257
Relationship-specific investments, 258
Repetition, in oligopoly, 188, 202–208
Reputation, leveraging, 324. *See also* Game theory
Re-sale, preventing, 268
Resource allocation, 356–357, 367–371
  in corporate strategy process, 401
    financial capital, 367–369
    human capital, 369–371
    personnel evaluation and, 378
Ricoh, 303
R.J. Reynolds, 212, 358
RJR Nabisco, 212, 358
Robinson-Patman Act, 268–269
Rodrik, Dani, 342
Rolls Royce, 58
Ross, David, 213n
Rotemberg, Julio, 207n
Routines
  defined, 76
  for information and influence, 373–375
  interfaces for, 87–88
  for intervention, 375–377
  nature of, 86–87
Rule of squares, 308n
Rumelt, Richard P., 122n

S

Saatchi and Saatchi, 120
Saloner, Garth, 101n, 207n
Samuel Adams, 159, 161
Saturn division (GM), 2, 160–161, 171, 299
Scenario analysis, 301–302
Scherer, F. Michael, 213n, 360n
Schmalensee, Richard, 122n
Schumpeter, Joseph, 279, 279n, 294, 304
Schwinn, 291, 293
Scope of business, 21, 382
Scott Morton, Fiona, 213n
Screening. *See* Game theory
Seagate Technology, 298, 299
Secure Digital Music Initiative (SDMI), 326
Sega, 93
Self-enforcing agreements, 204
Senior management
  and business development function, 115
  compensation and, 83
  and strategy process, 382–383, 396
Shapiro, Carl, 313n
Sherman Act, 211–213, 236–237
Shimano, 292
Signaling
  as entry barrier, 235–236
  nature of, 200–202. *See also* Game theory
Silicon Graphics, 101
Simple market transactions, 256–257
Sony Corporation, 46, 47, 49, 85, 101, 325, 362–363
Southwest Airlines, 67–71, 73, 88–89, 97–100, 387–388
Specialization, 77, 290, 293
Spectrum of competition, 150–154
  dominant firm, 151, 152–153, 154, 209–210
  monopoly, 150–152, 154, 173–176, 247–249
  niche markets, 151, 152, 154–157, 163–165, 178–183, 315–317

Spectrum of competition *(continued)*
  oligopoly. *See* Oligopoly
  perfect competition, 151, 152, 176–178
Sprint, 57
Standardization
  compatibility benefits of, 306–308
  de facto standards, 45, 326–327
  de jure standards, 327
  open standard, 325
  standards-setting process, 326–328
Standard Oil, 7
Status, and positional advantage, 45
Stern, Scott, 163n
Stevenson, Howard H., 48, 48n
Stigler, George, 290n
Strategic alignment, 95–101
  components of, 95–97
  other examples of, 101
  at Southwest Airlines, 97–100
Strategic alliances, 7–8
Strategic groups, niche markets and, 163–165
Strategic management, 1–2
  goals of, 3–4
  nature of strategy and, 4
  role of business strategy and, 2–10
Strategic planning, 8–10
  problems of, 9–10
  strategic thinking versus, 8–10, 382
  in strategy process, 8–9, 15, 383, 390–392
Strategic spillovers, 354–356, 358, 361–366
  identifying and managing, 362–363
  sources of, 363–366
Strategic thinking
  requirements of, 12
  strategic planning versus, 8–10, 382
Strategic uncertainty, 281
Strategy process, 8–9, 381–403
  autonomous, 381, 395–397
  business strategy, 33–38, 383–390
  corporate strategy, 397–403
    role of general manager, 402–403
    for strategically independent businesses, 398–401
    for strategically interdependent businesses, 401–402
  evolution of strategy in, 389–390, 393–397
  intentional, 381, 395–397
  principles of, 382–383
  selecting and communicating strategy, 388–389
  of Southwest Airlines, 67–71, 387–388
  strategic change and, 36–38, 271–304, 389–390
  strategic plans in, 8–10, 15, 382, 383, 390–392
  strategy evaluation in, 35–36, 385–388
  strategy identification in, 34–35, 384–385
Strategy statement, 28–32
  benefits of, 29–30
  example of, 31–32
  form and use of, 30–31
Structure-Conduct-Performance (SCP) paradigm, 124–127
Stulz, Rene M., 359n
Substitutes
  industry definition based on "close," 145–146
  Justice Department definition of, 145–146
  nature of, 131–132
Sunk costs, incumbency advantage from, 229
Sun Microsystems, 326, 361
Sunrise Medical, charter of, 24–25
Supplier power, 245n
  bargaining with powerful buyers, 251–254
  change and, 276
  in Structure-Conduct-Performance (SCP) paradigm, 126–127
  value capture and, 247–254
  in value chain analysis, 142, 243–244
  vertical power, 140–142

Sustainable competitive advantage, 48–51
Swatch, 335
Switching costs
   and demand-side increasing returns, 312–313, 317
   incumbency advantage from, 227
   sources of, 227–228
SWOT analysis, 35–36

T
Tall organization, 79
Task forces, 81
Teams, 81
Technological uncertainty, 280
Technology adoption, 321–326
   bandwagon effect, 322, 323
   early adopters, 323
   expectations, 323
   intermediate adopters, 323
   managing, 323–326
Teece, David, 274n
3Com, 358
360 degree evaluation, 84–85
3M Corporation, 7–8, 85, 105, 109, 112, 114, 383
Tightly coupled organizations, 82, 106–109
Time Warner, 235, 256
Timing, in oligopoly, 188, 197–199
Tipping, 311–315
Top-down approach, 16
Toyota, 171, 256–257, 260, 344–345
Training, switching costs of, 227
Trajtenberg, Manual, 39n, 163n
Transaction costs, 258
   switching costs of, 227–228, 312–313, 317
Transfer prices, 85
Transnational corporation, 348–349
Treaty of Rome, 213
Turner Broadcasting, 235, 256
Tushman, Michael L., 296n

U
Uncertainty
   in emerging markets, 278–282
   of product quality, 226–227
   scenario analysis and, 301–302
Unilever, 344
U.S. Steel, 7, 206, 211

V
Value
   adding, 358–361, 368–369, 383
   and competitive advantage, 39–40
Value-based corporate strategy, 369
Value capture, 244–255
   without buyer or supplier power, 245–247
   through dividing potential industry earnings (PIE), 136, 142–144
   in industry analysis, 136
   reducing power in other segments and, 254–255
   by single powerful supplier (or buyer), 247–249
   and value creation, 239–242
   when buyers and suppliers are powerful, 249–254
Value chain, 127–144
   buyer power in, 143, 244
   competition in, 136–138, 139–140, 142
   entry and incumbency advantage in, 138–140
   entry barriers in, 138–140, 142
   examples of, 128–129, 133–136, 139–140, 142–144, 242–243
   nature of, 127–128
   supplier power in, 142, 243–244
   value capture in, 136, 142–144
   value creation in, 129–136
   vertical power in, 140–142
Value creation, 255–263
   without buyer or supplier power, 246
   coordination problem in, 257–260
   example of, 133–136

incentive problem in, 260–263
potential industry earnings (PIE) and, 129–136, 274–276
with single monopolist, 248
and value capture, 239–242
Values statement, 26–27
Variable costs, 217
Varian, Hal, 313n
Variation, selection, and retention (VSR), 105–106, 345
Vertical communication, 343–344
Vertical differentiation, 161–162
Vertical foreclosure, 235
Vertical integration, to prevent re-sale, 268
Vertical organization, of industry, 287–292
Vertical power, in value chain analysis, 140–142
Vision, 27, 391

W
Wages, productivity and, 341–342
Wal-Mart, 45, 102, 170–171, 227, 241–242, 260
Walt Disney Corporation, 24, 50, 354–356, 358, 376
Wayland, Rebecca E., 347
Welch, Jack, 11, 378
Wernerfeld, Birger, 53, 53n
Whinston, Michael, 139n
Wiersema, Fred, 68n
Winter, Sidney., 15n
World Trade Organization (WTO), 334–335
World Wide Web, 310

X
Xerox Corporation, 8, 52, 85, 116, 302–304

Z
Zilog, 305